IN PURSUIT OF THE
ABOMINABLE SNOWMAN

In Pursuit of the
ABOMINABLE SNOWMAN

Odette Tchernine

TAPLINGER PUBLISHING COMPANY
NEW YORK

First Published in the United States in 1971 by
TAPLINGER PUBLISHING CO., INC.
New York, New York

International Standard Book Number 0-8008-4187-5

Library of Congress Catalog Card Number 75-147809

Printed in the United States of America

Acknowledgments

Without Doctor Boris Porshnev, the Russian Historian and Scientist, of the U.S.S.R. Academy of Sciences, permitting me to use his records of almost a lifetime spent in investigating the same question as dealt with in my present book, it would have taken me very much longer to complete this final version.

I thank him most gratefully for his generosity, and am happy to be in a position to tell of his long efforts for some truths to be more widely known.

My similar expressions of thanks go to Professor Doctor Rinchen, of the Mongolian Academy of Science, who also provided me with equally valuable material regarding the Snowman/Almas situation, which includes not only records of his own endeavours, but of former scientists and scholars before his time who for many years had tried to fill in the gaps in information.

Gordon W. Creighton, M.A., F.R.A.I., F.R.G.S., of H.M. Diplomatic Service, Retired, now with the Permanent Committee on Geographical Names, Royal Geographical Society, has given me the advantage of his knowledge by translating Russian texts for me, as I do not speak that language, and translating terms and place-names beyond the Russian borders from the Chinese, Tibetan, and Mongolian languages. My thanks and great appreciation for such help go to him.

I express thanks to Doctor K. Ramamurti, Postal Adviser to the Kingdom of Bhutan for valuable data, and specimens of that country's recent beautiful stamps, also for his asking me some time ago for copies of my previous writings to lodge in their Postal Library. I cannot let this pass without my mentioning my appreciation to His Majesty King Jigme Dorji Wangchuk for accepting copies also of my books, to which, with his permission, I hope to add this present one.

A thank you to Rear-Admiral Vernon Donaldson because he was the one who most helpfully directed me how to find a story called The Ngoloko which has connotations with this book's subject matter. I also thank Messrs William Blackwood and Sons Ltd., for allowing me to quote excerpts from The Ngoloko by J. C. Elliot, published originally in the 1917 November number of Blackwood's Magazine. I had some interesting sidelights on this story from Colonel R. G. Bulkeley Lynn-Allen, and also his permission to publish his own story dealing with the same African territory of this story which he knew well, and where a white hunter friend of his had a mystery encounter with an unidentified upright-walking being.

Acknowledgments and thanks go to Mr Angus McDonald who gave me the account of the mystery creature that attacked him several years ago when he and fellow-engineers were engaged in rail opening up of unexplored country in East Africa.

Lord Medway, anthropologist and zoologist, sent me an account a few years ago about what was obviously the Borneo version of the Snowman theme. If he ever reads this book, he will see that I have now been able to quote his anecdote. When he sent it to me before, delaying communications between remote parts of the Far East and Britain made it impossible for me to include it in my previous Snowman book which was already being printed. Thank you, Lord Medway, for an original and pleasing true story.

Finally, I am much indebted to the Polish sculptor-anthropologist, Wienczyslaw Plawinski, for the photograph of Professor Rinchen and himself, and for the photographs showing his reconstruction work on the Almas skull.

Introduction

Thinking about it, I don't write, I wrestle. Books are worried out of places, news, and people, and are pounded out side by side with the pounding out of the other thing, my other daily livelihood of words.

My previous book, *The Snowman and Company* was a tough, and some thought, a ridiculous search. This one is its logical continuation; new facts, and very occasional laughter. Some of the situations that occur in a book of this nature call for this exercise.

Is it a saving grace? I don't know. All I do know is that it has saved me from disgracing myself in moments of terror which have nothing to do with the present pages.

This pilgrimage taken to follow up the Snowman into paths of what some will call incredible fact, had gaps in information, blank spaces, lost or derided causes to worry out, silences to explain, and contradictions to account for.

And also a few nonsense stories which I always quote so as to discredit them, and to evoke that saving smile.

The book is an attempt to extricate again, contemporarily, the truth about a phenomenon of nature's history that has been ignored and played down for centuries. I have tried to co-ordinate the scattered history of certain rare living creatures. The results are presented step by step as information unfolded from my hammering out through legend, superstition, deceit, fear, and FACT. Knowledge came, not in carefully compiled documentation, but from far-flung sources and unexpected news.

Nature is unpredictable and uneven. Seeds fall, marking unusual trails, and nature laughs at cultivation. I had to follow those trails of growth and their side-shoots.

This book is torn from the rock of ages and the edges of its substance may read roughly.

I owe a great deal to those who have travelled with me part of the way in the search, and to whom I give thanks on another page.

Odette Tchernine

Contents

CHAPTER ONE

An Ice Mystery, or Murder?

While I was halfway through this ultra-zoological survey, during the spring of 1969, the showman, Frank Hansen of U.S.A., produced a mystery creature—a dead one. Hansen stated that the mysterious hairy body had been found preserved in a lump of ice in the Bering Straits. On a subsequent occasion came a statement that the specimen had been bought in Hongkong, with no reason given for this contradiction in terms.

Doctor Bernard Heuvelmans, the Belgian scientist, and author-scientist Ivan Sanderson examined the remains through glass. Other scientists were alerted, among them Dr John Napier who had taken part in the Californian *Bigfoot* television documentary some time earlier. Once more since the Bigfoot incident (which will figure in a later chapter) anthropologists were faced with a problem. Was the somewhat ape-like, hirsute, ice-encased specimen, which showed signs of modern injury, a sample of pre-history as claimed at first by the showman, and how had it got into the ice? Was this a hoax, or was it crime?

The Federal Bureau of Investigation of America were alleged to be watching.

Ivan Sanderson and Bernard Heuvelmans pressed on in their enquiries, and some very curious facts came to light. For a start, Heuvelmans had written a paper on the case for the "Bulletin of the Royal Institute of Natural Sciences" of Belgium, several months before the mystery of the "Iceman" became more known. He called his thesis "Preliminary Note on a Specimen preserved in the ice; an unknown *living hominid*", [*The italics are mine*] and I suggest that by the term "living" Dr Heuvelmans means a specimen that could be equated with a currently recognised type of man.

American opinion does not consider this specimen entirely an Abominable Snowman type, though this is open to query.

The feature which amazes the investigators is that this thing from the ice has been on exhibition in carnivals and fairs for two years, during which thousands of people have seen it, paying twenty-five cents for the viewing, and nobody, save one person questioned its nature.

The notice against its show case stated: *Possibly a mediaeval man left over from the ice age.* Note the contradictory terms which show a definite lack of interest in accuracy.

Hansen asked Doctor Heuvelmans and Ivan Sanderson to keep quiet on whatever it was they discovered about the specimen until permission for them to speak out was given by the owner. The owner was supposed to be a prominent and eccentric rich man living in California. Heuvelmans, and Sanderson would not promise, and, according to Sanderson, the owner, or owners, of the Iceman refused to answer any questions on its origin and history.

In spite of their non-cooperation, Heuvelmans circulated his thesis among leading anthropologists. All agreed that the specimen was an authentic type of man.

What type?

It was then that the matter was referred to the American authorities. They put the same question to Hansen, who was probably the person who had first leaked the news of the Iceman's discovery. Again he refused to reply. But when these official enquiries began, the owner came to Minnesota where his "property" lay in storage, and took it away in a refrigerated truck. He left behind a sort of duplicate of the figure made out of wax.

The reason for official alerting was because by now suspicions were aroused. It might have been that the so-called Iceman was a human primitive whom someone had confronted in one of the wildest parts of the American mountains. The mystery of the whole affair might have begun just there, as a trick by a person or persons to dispose of an incriminating corpse. Signs of modern injuries had been discovered on the remains, and such evidence

2

could indicate such a crime.

Then the investigators found that the specimen had been hidden for a year, even before its ice-bound travels around the showgrounds, and that when the eccentric owner first obtained it he went to great lengths to hide it.

Of all the hundreds of people who saw the specimen when it was on show, there was only one really interested onlooker, Perry Cullen, a herpetologist and naturalist from Milwaukee. It was he who drew the attention of Sanderson and his colleagues.

Sanderson later stated that when "Bozo", as he nicknamed the Iceman, has been sorted out, it would be useless to argue against the Darwinian theory. He made crytic references to the Old Testament and said that the best guide to a new understanding of mankind would be to re-read it, preferably in an edition as near as possible to the original old Hebraic or Aramaic. If one looked back to "this ancient pragmatic exercise in clear thinking" one would get an explanation of "just what poor Bozo most likely is".

Genesis in Chapter Six makes reference to a race of giants who "married the daughters of men". In the Hebrew language these giants were known as the "Nephilim", which means a race of big people. *Genesis* One in that chapter states: "And it came to pass, when men began to multiply on the face of the earth, and daughters were born unto them." *Genesis* Two continues: "That the *sons of God* saw the daughters of men that they were fair, and they took them wives of all which they chose". And continuing—"There were giants on the earth in those days, and also after that when the sons of God came in unto the daughters of men, and they bare children to them, the same became mighty men which were of old, men of renown. . . ."

Could that strange Transatlantic search for the truth about Bozo be explained by reading between the lines of these ancient words? Could part of the answer to other human or semi-human riddles, with which the Iceman mystery might be associated, begin just here too?

Was the unusual discovery genuine, was it after all a remnant of pre-history, or some freakishly hirsute being of the present age who had suffered an extraordinary fate? Or was this a drifted specimen illustrating the vexed Snowman/*Almas* question.

Much of Bernard Heuvelman's current views tally with the first Iceman factors, but there were new and recent details which justified a re-examination of the case.

Perry Cullen alerted the experts, and the additional factors stemmed from there.

After referring to the fairground showings for the benefit of a French enquiry, Heuvelmans recalled how the Iceman was alleged to have been found in the floating block of ice.

In view of the geographical location of the find, I have wondered if the creature might perhaps have been of *Ainu* origin; a postulation afterwards recorded having been put forward by one of the scientists interviewed.

French sources stated that a Soviet ship found the body and was forced to put in at a Chinese port where their cargo, including the ice-cased specimen was confiscated. Bozo vanished for several months, to re-appear as a piece of contraband curiosity in Hongkong. This was said to be where its anonymous owner had first acquired it. Mr Cullen's secretary had tried diligently to discover the name and address of the unknown purchaser, but failed. The only news available had been what my own enquiries had extricated, that he had been in Minnesota, and then disappeared.

It was at this point that Frank Hansen agreed to see Heuvelmans and Sanderson. The interview took place on 17 December, 1968, producing a variation of information. A different version of the finding of the Iceman was that it had been fished out of the sea by Japanese whalers. Hansen then said that the owner, who had bought Bozo, was a film tycoon, a Californian travelling around in the East searching for interesting curios to use for scenic effects.

This man must have been the anonymous personage whose name Hansen had been enjoined to keep secret, and who had rewarded him financially for putting the Iceman on show. They were supposed to have shared the profits of this peep-show.

The foregone has a slightly Munchausen flavour, but one

must remember that the unknown Californian was reputed to be eccentric as well as rich.

Doctor Heuvelmans gave an amplified description of the ice-bound thing. It was displayed on a sort of trailer, this in its turn supporting a huge refrigerated coffin, measuring 2.20 metres in length by 20 centimetres in width. The container was lighted from within by fluorescent tubes. A large layer of thick glass acted as lid. Hansen told Heuvelmans and Sanderson that the ice block itself at the time of acquisition measured approximately 2.75 metres long, by 1.50 metres wide, and 1.20 metres in height. It weighed some 2.700 kilos. To ensure the best visibility the ice block had been substantially reduced.

"The specimen resembled a man, yet, seemed "non-human" because it did not correspond entirely to man's actual definitions. To add to the mystery, this specimen which was nearer to Neanderthal specifications, had been killed by a firearm.

The Belgian professor's analysis after having examined it through the glass carries value in view of his reputation in the fields of anthropological and allied sciences: He said:

"The specimen at first sight is representative of man or pre-ferably, the description at the first stage could be an adult human of masculine sex. Height 1 metre 80 centimetres. Of fairly normal proportions, but excessively hairy. Except for the face, the palms of the hands, soles of the feet, the penis and testicles, the creature is entirely covered with very dark brown hair, of seven to ten centimetres long. His skin is of the wax-like colour characteristic of corpses of men of white race when not tanned by the sun.

"This is detectable over the whole body, more particularly outside the frankly hairless zones, such as the chest centre, and the knees. Hairs were more separated on other body parts. Altogether, the hair situation reminds one of a chimpanzee's fur, and not, for instance, the dense fur of a bear.

"The damage to the occiput [back of the head], and the fact that the eyeballs had been ejected from their sockets, one

5

having completely disappeared, suggests that the creature had been shot in the face by several large-calibre bullets. One bullet must have penetrated the cubitus [forearm] when he tried to protect himself. A second bullet pierced the right eye, destroying it, and causing the other to start out of its cavity. This caused the much larger cavity at the back of the cranium, producing immediate death."

Hansen had shown the Iceman at fairgrounds since the third of May, 1967. As the specimen was decomposing in parts, he had intended showing it for only one more year before authorising an autopsy. This is a peculiar report in view of the first Iceman news suggesting that there might be suspicion of foul play, and that the authorities might in any case wish to examine the mystery. If this occurred, it would take place with or without permission of the man in charge.

Immediately Hansen's plan was known, Heuvelmans and Sanderson proposed to purchase the specimen. Negotiations were in progress when the new sensation of the Iceman vanishing frustrated their aims.

Reports of the curious story increased in several countries. One foreign report gave a variation of the ice block's world travels, that it had been sold to an unknown party who had removed it to an unknown destination. Just another version of previous reports.

All that remained was the evidence of Heuvelmans and Sanderson, arrived at on the spot, their photographs of the Iceman in his cold prison, and his reconsructed image drawn by Heuvelmans.

I believe my first report of the Iceman disappearing is the correct solution. Everything points to the purchaser being none other than the original owner himself.

Bernard Heuvelmans consulted Jack Arthur Ullrich of Westport, New Jersey, who is a geological specialist, a hydrologist, and glaciologist. Their conversation, according to the best of my enquiries on this complicated Snowman-related case, circled mostly on ice conditions relating to preservation. Asked how

6

long he thought the specimen could have been preserved in natural ice, Ullrich said that the rapidity with which decomposition set in would depend on the current temperature.

Temperature can be lowered artificially, so that all putrefaction is practically arrested, but such intense cold is nonexistent on our planet. No animal such as a mammoth or any other prehistoric beast, has ever been preserved naturally in ice. In Siberia, mammoths and woolly rhinocerii have been discovered in muddy swamp terrain. But this might be due to formation of tannic acid which has the tendency to preserve from corruption. The temperature alone of natural ice can only retard the process of decay, but cannot prevent it eventually.

Opinion now was that the age of the Iceman specimen was only a few years.

Was the creature's present state the result of a natural accident after immersion in an icy sea, or was it refrigerated artificially after it had been dredged out? Ullrich thought that natural ice-preservation in this case was extremely unlikely. For this to have occurred the corpse would have had to sink in the water without dropping immediately to the bottom of the sea bed, and for the water to congeal while enveloping the body, before the body was devoured by predators or decomposed by bacteria. A body thus congealing would accumulate over its whole surface a film of irregular ice layers. The present specimen being encased in very clear ice could not have become congealed in the sea, but was later refrigerated artificially.

Here was no fossil either. Mr Ullrich's conjectures on the specimen's nature when alive discounted the proposition that Bozo was an ape-man conserved in natural ice down the ages. He suggested, as previously propounded, that it might have been a human individual, abnormal perhaps, but of our own species.

Could there be a connotation there after all with the Hairy Ainu, the specimen being a lost representative of that fast-disappearing but known race? On the other hand, does *he* indicate simply a "phoney", a manufactured model, a composite thing, though this seems almost physically impossible.

To all questions, Bernard Heuvelmans' views seem rational

7

enough, and others share them; that there might still be Neanderthal men, more ancient than all men, that live among us.

And one such Neanderthal man had been killed by shots from a gun, and at close range. It is possible that Heuvelmans' and Sanderson's current investigations have major interest. Somewhere on earth men-relics from the Neanderthal Age still exist. Somewhere these men co-exist with ordinary human beings, one of whom either out of panic or sheer destructive instinct used a firearm.

Somewhere? But where?

The northern Japanese Islands have been well scoured for one of the answers to such mysteries. In China there remain mysteries of unusual living beings in remote areas. But China would never have allowed a rare specimen like the Iceman to leave her territory knowingly.

Heuvelmans considers that if the creature that is still causing controversy in certain science circles in America was truthfully found floating in a block of ice in the Bering Straits or Sea, one must study any hypotheses on its origin. In addition to the remotely possible *Ainu* idea, it could have lived in British Columbia, in other far wilds of Northern Canada, in Alaska, or even in the back blocks of the United States. Hairy men have been reported from many parts of the world where a civilization has not yet encroached. Russia is another and important example. Doctor Boris Porshnev, the well-known Russian historian and scientist, has for years studied cases of small lost groups in the Caucasus and Siberia.

The venerable Professor Rinchen of Mongolia has been studying the question of hominid-remnants for a lifetime.

Certain discoveries are bound to upset both proved and preconceived facts of knowledge; all that we believe we know.

Bernard Heuvelmans has said that this question might resolve into being the most important discovery of our times.

One must remember the timidity of many scientific experts. From a French viewpoint the question of mysterious, non-recognised creatures receives a cold reception in British scientific

8

circles. But I do not think this is entirely true. Great caution does exist before a final commitment, but that is not exclusive to the official British attitude. This book will show how timidly, and often with hostility, other countries' "establishments" reacted for far longer than a mere one hundred years.

*   *   *

In my introduction I said how my work resolves into a wrestling match. Here are two bouts that must be added to this chapter which came to light when the whole material was already in process of preparing for publication.

Professor Bernard Heuvelmans' conversations with Frank Hansen were now amplified. He met him again at Hansen's home in Rollingstone, Winona County, Minnesota, where Hansen repeated statements he had made, but now said he had no idea of the Iceman's nature. He said it was even possible that the specimen was only a clever oriental fabrication, like so-called *mermaids* sold in the main ports of the Indian Ocean as curiosities. They are generally the product of a very complicated assembly of a monkey's body or a lemur's, a fish tail, and the claws of a predatory bird. This last physical trait has never been attributed to the mermaid's legendary image. Probably the idea is to create something sensational. It could well be that whoever first saw the disputed ice specimen was looking for artificial "Monster" exhibits to commercialise in the U.S.A.)

Perhaps the fact of Hansen now casting doubts on the macabre contents of his showcase having ever been genuine is an opting-out of responsibility because he may think a showdown is inevitable. Such an assumption seems reasonable, especially as a slight scent of decay was beginning to escape from one corner of the coffin, even though it was closed. And one of the toes showed a change of colour which Hansen himself admitted having noticed. He stated that he could continue showing the specimen for another year, but feared such a delay would cause decay beyond the point when a scientific study in depth could be applied.

Professor Heuvelmans pursued the case with several hypotheses. Firstly, he said the object could have been entirely artificial. But this he rejected as impossible. Next, it could be a composite assembly of spare parts taken from divers species. That too he rejected. Thirdly, it could be an individual belonging to some known race of *Homo Sapiens*. There was doubt there too. Fourthly, it might be an abnormal human freak. The fifth suggestion was that the Iceman was of a race, or sub-race, of Man still unknown. The sixth hypothesis indicated an entirely different species of Man. Heuvelmans suggested that the theory of a specimen of an unknown race of Man was just possible. All races have thrown up freakishly hairy samples from time to time.

At this point the Professor quoted the American anthropologist, Carleton Coon. Apparently this scientist's book, "Origin of Races" (published in 1912), describes the Ainus "as hirsute as a hairy Scot or Jew". I cannot quite see why those two particular races were picked out as displaying extreme hairiness. Professor Heuvelmans, speaking in all seriousness, stated that the Iceman was much, much more hirsute! Still, there have been exceptionally hairy human beings known to medical history down the centuries. Such records appear in "Les Velus" ("The Hirsute Ones") a book written in 1912 by Doctors Le Double and Houssay.

With due respect to Professor Heuvelmans, the Iceman hypothesis of a fabricated specimen, which he rejected, is the one I have always been inclined to favour since the beginning of this strange story of a creature dredged up from ice.

The following final piece of information to reach me almost confirms my view.

Like many investigators, I play my hunches. One of these, some months ago, was that some Vancouver records would contain a clue to the mystery; so I wrote to find out. After some weeks, only a few days after receiving the amplified Heuvelmans data, I received a report from Mr J. N. Lewis, of the Press Library, Vancouver. He had just discovered the clue, and it had appeared in the *Vancouver Sun* on May 10th, 1969. The implication was that the Iceman was a fake. That same month, the Smithsonian Institution of U.S.A. indicated that the specimen being exhibited up and down the United States was an artificial shape composed of latex rubber and hair.

George Berklacy of the Smithsonian, stated that he had been in touch with a Californian wax museum owner who told him that one of his employees had worked on the Iceman in the spring of 1967 inserting hair into the latex rubber body. This tallies with the time Frank Hansen began showing his "prehistoric" specimen at fair grounds. The museum owner would not disclose the name of the man who had performed the exhausting task of covering the shape with millions of hairs. The indication of decay escaping from the Iceman's glass case does not constitute a contradiction. A non-human substance like rubber can be equally objectionable when deteriorating.

Doctor John Napier, chief of the primatology department at the Smithsonian, and eminent in his field, was curious, but Frank Hansen refused to let him examine the exhibit closely, just as he had refused others.

Doctor Napier said that the chances now seem pretty high that the Iceman was merely a fabricated model. But he is still interested and wishes he could have examined it. He added that it was difficult to believe that Heuvelmans could have been fooled so easily.

Though now it is practically certain that the Iceman is a piece of trickery, one is bound to agree with John Napier.

And that is why this first chapter begins with the story of a probable hoax. Because, supposing there was one fragment of truth in this involved and often absurd story, some of its features do equate with this book's theme of the Snowman-plus-Neanderthal situation. And also because if the Iceman is a complete hoax, as I am almost certain it is, fabrications of this nature must be exposed so as to prevent their perpetuation.

Finally a closing statement. The Federal Bureau of Investigation, Washington, D.C. have been good enough to advise me that they have no information to send me regarding the "Iceman", "Nor has this Bureau taken any part in investigation in connection with this case". The letter is written at the highest level, and the signature represents a living and legendary name.

CHAPTER TWO

Re-assessing Snowman History

My first book on this theme. *The Snowman and Company* ended with an old folk saying from India that had been quoted to me: "One day as I was walking on the mountainside, I saw at a distance what I thought to be a beast. As I came closer I saw it was a man. As I came closer still I found it was my brother."

The present record of a renewed search begins with the final words of the last one.

In the light of contemporary and so far little known developments (*circa* 1968) that fragment from Indian folklore might have been prophetic without my entirely realising its nature at the time of quoting.

My former work mentioned at the beginning of this chapter was a survey covering two-thousand years of continuous if sporadic records and references to the Abominable Snowman's mysterious history.

There have been rare sightings, evidence, and photographs of footprints in the Himalaya and elsewhere. The most notable Himalayan ones were those Eric Shipton took on the Menlung Glacier in 1951 when on his Everest Reconaissance expedition.

The Snowman or Yeti was for many years considered to be distributed, if it existed at all, only in the Himalaya and in Tibet. On various explorations down the years mountaineers brought back stories of Snowmen raids at seldom explored altitudes, and around isolated lama monasteries. I reported most of the sightings, sounds, and incidents relating to the creature's presence, from Nepal, the Karakoram, Kashmir, Sikkim, and the once practically unknown kingdom of Bhutan. Included in this first collection were the legends, superstitions, and nonsense stories, presented so as to give the reader opportunity to separate the

12

grain from the chaff.

Whenever some new report brought news of the Snowman into prominence, the majority of scientists, anthropologists, and zoologists refused to accept the possibility of an unknown species existing. In their opinion, rare sightings, sounds, depredations and footprints were merely evidence of the presence or recognised fauna. The chief candidates for this explanation were the bear and the ape.

Many of the Yeti stories came from local people. For instance, in several cases from the Sherpas, those tough mountain élite whose expert familiarity with the high altitudes helped the numerous well-known climbers who led some of the most famous mountaineering expeditions in the world. The lamas of the various solitary monasteries and cliff-hanging gömpas (temples), also supplied interesting if somewhat debatable evidence of knowledge of the Yeti and its haunts and habits. Relics of supposed skins and scalps were produced, and brought back to Britain for examination by experts. More often than not the lama evidence was rightfully inadmissible after minutely carried out experiments. But in some cases sparse tufts of hair defied the microscope and other tests, for they could not be identified with the hairs of any accepted animal.

I was once played back a tape-recording taken by a friend of mine who was conveying my interrogatory messages to a slightly notorious lama in Nepal. She was able to catch on that tape the rather spine-chilling story of a kidnapping told her by the lama's daughter. Years before when she was very young, a girl she knew had been carried off to the high altitudes by a Yeti. That tape was quite a curiosity. It may still be in my reporter friend's possession.

In 1921, Colonel C. K. Howard-Bury, the leader of an Everest expedition, reported coming across large footprints that looked human, where to his knowledge no other humans had ventured before. This was on the Lhakpa La, a 21,000 feet pass north-east of the mountain. His porters told him that the tracks were those of "The wild men of the snows". The colonel cabled this back to civilisation more as a joke than a fact, but his report created a sensation and was taken seriously. The Abominable Snowman controversy had started.

Later it was learnt that the so-called "wild men" were known as the *Metch-Kangmi*. *Kang* means *snow* in Tibetan, spoken in Nepal, Sikkim and some other regions as well as in Tibet and Bhutan, and *mi* means *man*. As for the term *Metch*, some confusion occurred, and I believe, still occurs. It was first translated as *Abominable*. Some experts in theTibetan and other languages then took a hand in the argument, and stated that they thought *metch* might mean *disgusting* or *ragged*. The first title clung. The Yeti has been popularly known as the Abominable Snowman ever since, though it is known too by other names in different localities. Among such we find: *Migö*; *Rakshi-Bompo*; *Bangjakri*; *Dremo*; all this according to various regions where fact and legend about it meet.

The year 1921 was not the date of the first reports. Continuous reference to the Snowman even appears under the name of Rakshi, or Rakshasa in *Rama and Sita*, one of India's national epics. Its best known version is ascribed to Sri Valmiki, a poet of the third or fourth century B.C. He is chiefly remembered for that saga of the tribulations of Prince Rama and his bride Sita in exile from their rightful kingdom. It was translated into English at the beginning of the twentieth century by Romesh Dutt.

During long research I came across a forgotten Himalayan travel book published in 1820. In one of its chapters dealing with rather tourist-like trips into Kashmir were notes on unidentifiable tracks of a mystery animal. The porters were perturbed, and said the tracks were made by a creature they called the *Bang* of which they stood in fear. This was obviously another name for the Yeti. The publication date of this book was many years before the Abominable Snowman was granted semi-official recognition as a debatable animal, if not a proved fact, and the 1820 reference in that book had not been discovered until I found it and published it in my own book *The Snowman and Company*.

In her comments on the mystery of the Himalayan Yeti, Mira Behn (Mahatma Gandhi's English disciple) once made a plea that if any proved sighting ever happened near enough for capture, there should be a gentle approach to "the unknown brother of the mountains". Later she told me about the Van Manas, or Ban Manas, the alleged Snowmen or "Forest Men" of the Garhwal in Northern India where she supervised high altitude cattle breeding for the Indian Government. She described the evidence of the herdsmen of the high Himalaya which tallied with sporadic Almas mysteries of the Russian outer wildernesses more than one hundred years ago, when the explorer Colonel Prjevalsky tried to elucidate their mystery, and was officially prevented from continuing. (Incidentally, Van or Ban means "Forest", and "Manas"—man. That is in Sanskrit and in its descended dialects like Hindi.)

Now, the Almas, or Snowman question in Russia has developed into a breakthrough which at the time of writing this is not generally known, and which is still progressing. The following pages will begin to amplify that progress and extend the very few records I could give in my last Snowman work.

In the last century Snowman search in Mongolia and elsewhere in the then Russian Empire by Prjevalsky brought his discoveries to an exciting climax. Governmental influences discouraged him from disclosing and publicising the results of his research. The government and the court hushed up reports of his work for fear of ridicule.

The Russians renewed scientific research in that field in the 1950's, as my previous book described. Then there seemed to be a shut-down on news. Some at the time thought this might be fear of ridicule again, following some strange reports from the mountains of the Pamirs. Now current circumstances suggest that the conspiracy of silence then was actually a veil to carry on work under cover without the outer world's curiosity.

So the 1950's report of a Pamirs sighting by a scientist called Pronin was mocked into silence, and even Doctor Boris Porshnev, the well-known scientist, must have been told to say no more.

Ridicule the world over is a potent weapon to arrest the exploring of the unknown and controversial. But the Russian derision of the 1950's had its purpose, the result of which is becoming apparent now in the knowledge of their consistent plodding in

15

the field. They took much interest at the time in Ralph Izzard's book describing how he and a band of experts went to the Himalaya in search of the Abominable Snowman, in an expedition elaborately mounted by a Fleet Street national newspaper. This was the expedition where tracks and general fauna-data were found, and valuable specimens and flora brought back, but where no actual Yeti were trailed.

Round about that time too some peculiar Northern Californian incidents were reported and attributed to Snowman or Bigfoot manifestations.

Those happenings were repeated in 1967 with even more details and resulted in a full-scale posse of scientists, zoologists and lay witnesses appearing in a television documentary. On the repetitive Californian story it is best to reserve judgment, though it will be examined more fully later on in these chapters.

The theory of the Himalayan (and the first known to the Western world) Snowman existence has so far been based on three suggested types of the creature: The very large type, vegetarian except when driven by great hunger and unable to find its usual feeding-stuff; the lesser-sized more aggressive predatory carnivore; and the small Rakshi-Bompo specimen, mischievous, raiding crops, and decamping when its presence is suspected.

I still hold a theory advanced in my earlier book. This is illustrated by my map drawing of what I call the S-Plan distribution, covering certain far-flung places on earth of similar nature where the Snowman phenomenon occurs from time to time (see p. 116). It may now be justified, especially in view of the new (to the West) revelations in the Russian sphere of exploration.

When I first began this new record, the Russian operations seemed engulfed in a repeated policy of non-communication. Then the little-known revelations were given to me in July 1968. In August of that year I tried to obtain more by making direct written approaches. Patience is always needed. I was rewarded, and at last a few more spheres of information opened up.

Contemporary Russian exploration took up in recent years where Prjevalsky of the nineteenth century was obliged to leave

16

off, and they have continued silently and undisturbed up till now. And it goes on.

The case now ties up right back with the *Almas*, the mystery creatures of the Mongolian wildernesses, and now of the Caucasus, the forest-covered mountains, valleys, and the deserts. It also has connotations with the *Van Manas* of the Garwhal and Kashmir high altitudes, as well as with the three-type Yeti of the Himalaya, associated with rare sightings, footprints, sights, and smells.

Three types? Will that number have to be revised in the light of new knowledge still to be proved and extended? The Russian field work could now point the way to a fourth type that one might ultimately call the first of the whole mysterious breed.

That fourth type might be allied to the Snowman image, or not at all, or it might bring the elucidation of the whole Snowman riddle.

The Russian field work might be on the point of revealing some very rare hominid distribution. What they have discovered and are studying might be primitive remnants of pre-history that have been able to pursue life undisturbed in the most impenetrable parts of the earth where the geographical background has been so far suitable for their survival.

Is this zoology, anthropology, or a hitherto unaccepted borderland mixture of both categories?

CHAPTER THREE

Little-known Russian Research Revealed

The current Russian field work, is taking place mainly in the Caucasus, in areas called Kabardinia and Balkaria. The leader of the recent expeditions is a woman scientist, Professor Jeanne Josefovna Kofman. Research has also been mounted in the Chatkal Range, a few miles east of Tashkent, and more than one expedition to investigate the Snowman, or *Almas*, has taken place in recent years.

Russian science papers on the expeditions aroused much interest. Since the first exploration began three hundred reports have reached Professor Kofman from eye-witnesses who have seen an unknown living entity, and who described footprints and other evidence. The descriptions of such sightings by country people, who farm in those remote and widely separated areas, more or less tally in detail.

Professor Kofman announced her findings at a lecture she gave in March 1966 at a Geographical Society in Moscow.

She had built up a mental picture of the unknown entity: the brow was low, narrow and backward-sloping, the nose small and flat as if pushed back, the chin was round and heavy, and the cheek bones high, and Mongolian in character. One other feature was stressed and that was the absence of a projecting chin, in spite of its alleged roundness.

From the skull reconstruction, assembled from several reports, emerges the likeness of a primate Hominid, but a very primitive one, suggesting a vanished type of *homo sapiens*. The Professor reminded her probably well informed listeners, with a Slavonic persistence in stressing detail, that from one feature correctly described a trained morphologist could re-create the picture of a whole creature.

18

The three hundred reports came from old peasants and tea-pickers on lonely mountain sites, and from people of every type and background. Reports came from widely separated places, told by persons who could not possibly know the assumptions and correlations formed by different experts. And yet every piece of scattered evidence tallies so that from the mass a clear image appears.

The Russian approach to this living riddle has some unusual and unconventional lines of enquiry that researchers in the West might not think of employing in a similar case. Criminal investigators were consulted, and they said that the evidence was enough to assemble an "identikit" portrait of the mystery creature on the findings in the reports.

Thirty per cent of the reports were dismissed. There are always lunatic fringe stories in such circumstances. But from the remainder of the evidence a recognisable type was produced.

Doctor Boris Porshnev is a famous historian of the Soviet Union, a scholar of wide learning, with doctorates in historical and philosophical sciences. He stated that for the first time in the history of his own Snowman investigations, here was data on remnant hominids. Probably the answer to the general "Snowman" mystery. Doctor Porshnev had often spoken on this subject before, basing assumptions on his own extensive knowledge and research with similarly interested colleagues. Now he felt justified to dissipate what he called "antiquated views expressed by contemporary anthropology", and he called for renewed discussion on a high scientific level.

Earlier, another well-known Russian expert, Professor Obruchev, changed his former non-committal approach to the subject, and asked that all *Almas* (Snowman) data be collected.

At the beginning of the field work only a few years ago, Professor Kofman said they were confronted with the unknown —what she called a "white patch on the map". That seems to have been an understatement in view of past sporadic research to clarify the mystery of Snowman, or Almas. Now however, she and her team were confident of great advance in their research.

Apparently, even the criminology experts engrossed in laboratory work, had with unconscious humour advised the Kofman group to "arrest the Almas". An order more easily voiced than achieved.

The Kofman team wanted to find out approximately what would be the population of the unknown species in that region of the Caucasus. Sightings were concentrated at first in a comparatively small area.

The team divided up a number of valleys where they planned to carry out a kind of census to estimate roughly how many were distributed there. They conducted daily observations in the Kuruko valley for several weeks. They came to the conclusion that an unknown living entity was there, not a domestic animal, not a man. There were thirty witnesses in one part of the valley alone. These included a group of children engaged in haymaking. The total of these local people had all seen X, as the creature was now called, and they all agreed that that particular X was a girl. In human terms she would be about sixteen. Witnesses had already sighted also a "tall thin man", another X with black hair fur. This one seemed to differ from other X's seen who were mostly red-haired.

These locals had been catching glimpses of the tall thin "man" for three years in succession at Dzhinale, a place ten kilometres from the Kuruko valley where the Kofman team were working. Around there too a fully grown female had been seen. A rather humourless report described how she had "impudently been visiting kitchen gardens close to the village".

Sightings also occurred at Nal'chik, the capital of Kabardinia. The Almas X observed there was thick-set and of medium height. He was seen near a river bank. He had just been frightened away by an old man with a gun who was protecting sunflower crops. The intruder had been raiding them. The elderly guardian had fired a shot, not to injure the trespasser, but to scare him away. Afterwards he remarked: "It was funny, just like a circus," when he told how the Almas had rushed off, threshing about in the sunflowers in his fright.

One day Professor Kofman's team discovered two lairs in tall, ordinarily impenetrable weeds. They found a heaped-up larder consisting of two pumpkins, eight potatoes, a half-chewed corn-cob, two thirds of a sunflower centre, blackberries, and the remains of three apples. Mixed up in this hoard were four round pellets of horse dung. It seems the Almas are very fond of this substance because of its salt content.

The investigators next found a section of a maize field where the Almas girl already mentioned had been searching for extra sweet cobs. She had first been biting them to test their sweetness, leaving tooth imprints, especially of the canines. Comparison with human imprints showed that the trespasser had a much wider jaw than the average human jaw. On the soil too were many imprints of flat, naked, inward-turning feet, characteristic of bow legs. Here there seemed to be remote association with my first Abominable Snowman research. There is a legend in the Himalaya that the Yeti possesses backward-turning feet to facilitate climbing steep altitudes. This story might have been a throw-back to racial memory of Orang-Utans, which, being arborial have inward-turning feet. Orangs have not been distributed in the Himalaya as far back as ordinary human memory can probe, but racial memory can at times be longer. Inward-turning characteristics could have been exaggerated to the term —backward-turning.

And those allegedly bow legs of the Almas suggests a contradictory term—anthropoid, or near-anthropoid.

In her most recent renewed expeditions Professor Kofman had some assistance and advice from an American, named Gerald Russell, versed in zoology and anthropology. He advised on the choice of essential equipment, such as lamps, flying syringes to fire sedatives, and other articles useful when camping in remote and difficult terrain.

The summer of 1967 weighed very hard on their field work. Bad weather had reduced their former base camp to a sorry quagmire, and there was much damage. The first month of their return to the area was entirely taken up in restoring the camp.

Then they were joined by a whole crowd of enthusiasts. That development seems almost incredible in view of the difficulties of

21

transport to such wild inaccessible regions. Thirty per cent of those well-meaning visitors were keen amateurs who had no knowledge that could make them of any use and they got in the way.

Nonetheless, several useful persons did take part in some of the Kofman expeditions. One was a retired man of some position from the Moscow area, and one was occupier of the Chair of Philosophy at Lvov. Some informed Moscow students joined in.

In Baku, a whole troop of teachers and schoolchildren became interested. Makarenko boarding-school went searching in the Talysh Mountains for clues. It is alleged that in those areas they found quite valuable data relating to "The Forest People", probably a local name for the *Almas*, who in some other regions are also called the *Kulieybani*. This led to the suggestion that here too in those remote mountains and forests hidden hominids from the past survived.

This term had already been mentioned in 1899. A great Russian geologist of his day, Professor K. A. Saturnin, related how he had encountered a female *Kulieybani*, and collected data on the "Forest People". He published a paper entitled *"Bianbanguli"*.

The second syllable in that rather tongue-twisting name is interesting. The *ban* or *bang* sound occurs in names given to similar mystery creatures in other parts of the world. In regions of the Himalaya and in Assam there used to be scatttred references to creatures called, "Bangjakri"—in other words, probably the eternal Snowman. Actually there is no linguistic connection. Similar sounds in speech occur the world over because the human tongue is only capable of a limited number of sounds.

"We are seeking a being of extraordinary nature," Professor Kofman is reputed to have stated on the renewal of *Almas* or X interest in Russia. She added that this being had been hidden for so long from them, not only because of history's own nature, but because of social and religious taboos.

There are still religious qualms about *Almas* X. The outbacks of Russia have many Moslems, and in the minds of some of them, especially in the case of older people, there is a confused image of the real but mysterious *Almas*—not a man, not an animal. They call those living apparitions, *Shaitan*, their name for Satan. To superstitious people in that part of the world, an *Almas* is a *Shaitan*.

It was not enough, said the Professor, to stress to those remote simple and superstitious people, that there are no Shaitans, because, as they say quite logically, they keep on meeting them. That could not be refuted. What was needed, she suggested, was not to deny the existence of the *Almas*, but only the perverted image of such creatures.

A difficult task of conversion, since the investigators themselves were not sure of the nature of the mystery being investigated.

Some local atheists in those regions who no doubt considered themselves very enlightened, took fright at the offer of a reward for the capture of an *Almas*. They were not afraid on humanitarian grounds that a caught *Almas* might get hurt. Not a bit of it. What they objected to was that, to quote their own words, such an offer amounted to *religious propaganda*. So fanatically committed were they to their brand of atheism that they demanded the Kofman expedition be terminated.

A rather inconclusive story was going around during that period about a certain Comrade L. from Sarmakov who met an Almas. He was so shaken by the mysterious and incomprehensible nature of the encounter that his nerves gave him some trouble. He consulted a doctor, but was only mocked for his state of mind, probably with a peculiar brand of Russian satire that can be devastating in its simplicity. So he went to a Moslem Mullah he knew. The old Moslem explained soothingly that the *Shaitan* was quite harmless. No need to fear it. Don't offend the *Shaitan*. That was the drill; so simple and easy. After that the neurotic chap lost his qualms. Comrade L. was reported to have told his friends: "I got quite well again. He's a very good Mullah."

CHAPTER FOUR

A Few Former Incidents

Long before the present Russian renewal in research, many scattered incidents occurred pointing to survival of the hairy "man-beast" in their unexplored regions.

Professor S. V. Obruchev, already mentioned, had expressed his views as an authoritative geographer in 1957 to a journalist of that decade who called himself L. Almazov [probably a form of humour—the word *Almaz* in Russian means a diamond], who was the Leningrad correspondent of the *Moscow Evening News*.

He quoted Professor Obruchev speaking at the Leningrad House of Scientists to an audience of eminent zoologists, geographers, biologists, and physiologists. The Professor said:

"The local inhabitants have long been giving reports about the 'Snowman'—in other words, the *Almas*—to European travellers. At the close of the last century, one of the British expeditions gave the first relatively clear and more precise reports of tracks of this being. In the course of the last sixty years, more than once travellers have seen these tracks in the snow, have measured and photographed them, but only once —in 1925—did a European traveller succeed in observing a 'snowman' and even then it was at a great distance."

An interruption is necessary here, for obviously Professor Obruchev was referring to A. M. Tombazi who, while about ten miles from the Zemu Glacier in the Himalaya, where other tracks have been seen, saw something living. This so far has been the only reliable eye-witness Himalayan-based evidence given by a European. Tombazi described the incident in a privately printed book

24

Footprints seen
by the 1951
Everest
Reconnaissance
and photographed
by Eric Shipton
on the
Menlung Glacier.

n individual
otprint at the
le of an ice axe.

Maps supplied by Plawinski. *Above*, part of Tibet showing places where Yeti discovered, marked with small "sputniks".

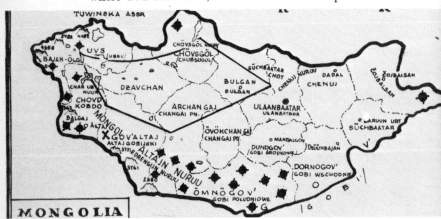

Above, where the Yeti is reported in Mongolia. *Below*, where reported in the Caucasus.

later on (A *Photographic Tour of Sikkim*) in which he wrote how his Sherpas called him from his tent and he saw the alleged Snowman. He wrote:

"Intense glare prevented my seeing anything for the first few seconds, but I soon spotted the object referred to. The figure outline was exactly like a human being, walking upright and stooping occasionally to uproot some dwarf rhododendrons. It showed dark against the snow and wore no clothing. Within the next minute it had moved in some thick scrub and disappeared. I examined the footprints which were similar in shape to those of a man but only six or seven inches long. Marks of five toes and instep were clear but trace of heel indistinct. The prints were undoubtedly those of a biped. From enquiries I gathered that no man had gone in this direction since the beginning of the year. The coolies naturally trotted out fantastic legends of Demons, Snowmen. Without in the least believing those delicious fairy-tales, notwithstanding the plausible yarns told by natives, I am at a loss to express any definite opinion. I can only reiterate with a sufficient degree of certainty that the silhouette of the mysterious being was identical with the outline of a human being."

The continued trend of Professor Obruchev's lecture spanned several years, and he went on:

"From January to May 1954 a special English expedition sought for the 'Snowman' in the Himalaya. The party consisted of four zoologists and anthropologists. Several times they found tracks in the snow, and as these were often fresh they tried to follow up the unknown creature, but did not succeed. It is true that the tracks permitted study of the animal's habits and to determine its zone of habitation.

"Putting aside all that is fantastic that was told to them about the Yeti, it is possible to reach the following conclusions: The animal goes mainly on two legs, but sometimes on all four limbs, for example in order to jump over crevasses in the ice.

25

The tracks are of various sizes and evidently belong to males, females, and young. The Snowman goes alone or in groups, but not more than four together.

"A portion of the reports in all probability are to be attributed to encounters with bears, but undoubtedly a portion relates to the anthropoidal Snowman."

Obruchev was no doubt quoting facts from the expedition in which Ralph Izzard took part, and which he wrote about in his 1955 book on that Himalayan adventure.

The Professor told his audience how descriptions of the Snowman tallied with those already known. The size was that of a young man, or even a grown man, the whole of him, apart from the face, covered with brown or grey fur or hair. He dwelt mostly between the upper forest line and the eternal snows, where his tracks are most easily followed. He lived on plants, grasses, berries, roots, insects, and small mammals. The Professor stressed the foot length of 25 to 30 centimetres. That coincides with the well-known measurements in English terms, of 12½ inches long, and roughly 6½ inches wide. A much wider foot than man's, Obruchev added, drawing attention to the very thick toe and second toes, clearly separated from the rest. That outline has long been established from the 1951 photograph taken by Eric Shipton.

Obruchev suggested that such a track combined the features of both man and ape, and was extremely similar to the footprints of the alleged first Stone Age Man, the Neanderthal man's imprint discovered in 1952 in caves in Italy. He gave the opinion that Snowman tracks were even more primitive.

The much discussed Yeti scalps were also referred to, described quite accurately as those that had been seen in a 1954 expedition in Himalayan monasteries where they had been kept as prized relics for more than 300 years. Though he gave their appearance with exactitude, the Professor did not deal with their suspect quality, probably he did not know of the European tests to which some of the artefacts had been subjected. Even as comparatively recently as in the 50's, world communications were not good between widely separated isolated areas. No doubt the lamas continue using the scalps at any ceremonials governmental changes allow, or they might have taken some of them away in exile.

In 1958 there was still local belief in parts of the Himalaya that remote regions harboured the mysterious anthropoid animal nearer to man than the gorilla and the chimpanzee, yet more primitive than the very earliest men of the stone age Establishing facts on the elusive being would always depend on catching a specimen alive. Great interest was aroused in Russia by the possibility of similar creatures being found within the limits of the U.S.S.R., say, the high regions of the Pamirs. The geographical terrain was similar. If the Snowman existed, in which *Almas* investigation was gradually hardening belief, the creature's long-established penetration from the main areas of distribution towards the North-West was possible.

Though the Pamirs inhabitants sometimes spoke of encounters with wild shaggy men, they did not at that time have precise data to settle the question firmly. But explorers and travellers visiting the high mountain regions of Russian Central Asia would in future have to study carefully all suspicious tracks they found, and try to collect well tested reports of the "*Galubyvan*" or *Gul'biyavan* as the "wild man" was called in the Pamirs.

January 22nd 1958 brought more facts to light, and a few did percolate to the western world, and then appeared to have been deliberately extinguished. More *Almas* or Snowman happenings occurred. They were sparsely mentioned in Western Europe and Britain where linguistic problems caused errors in translation as they can still do to this day, in spite of wider knowledge of the Russian language, and knowledge of the contrasts in Russia's varied continent. Perhaps also local inhabitants did not always produce needed evidence simply because communities in wild regions take sporadic strange sightings as a matter of course.

That year, "*Komsomol'skaya Pravda*" the organ of the Communist Youth Movement, reported how A. G. Pronin, whose name has been mentioned in a previous chapter, had seen a so-called Snowman. Pronin, a Leningrad hydrologist, had seen the

Snowman on the edge of a glacier in the Pamirs. This encounter was quoted in my earlier book, but it is only recently that Mr Pronin's full personal impression came my way, as he related it while describing briefly what he, Alexander Georgievitch Pronin, of the Geographical Scientific and Exploratory Institute of the Leningrad University, was doing there, as he led some hydrological work in those mountains. He said:

"After publication about 'Encounter with a Snowman' many people have come to me with dubious questions, and that is only natural. For indeed, could I make out, from a distance of 500 metres, whether that was in fact a so-called 'Snowman', or, as they call it, a '*Gul'biyavan*' and not, say, perhaps some other living creature? Naturally not. I am far from making a categorical affirmation. I just told the facts as they were, that is all. And a few inaccuracies in the press item have given my words a different meaning.

"How did it happen? Well, on August 11th, when selecting a site for our camp on the edge of the Fedchenko Glacier, I sent my fellow-workers with the horses to the settlement of Altyn-Mazar and remained alone. It was the peak time of the rainy season, and as a hydrologist, I had more than enough work to keep me busy. On August 12th at mid-day, I am following up a course of the valley of the river Balyandkiik, and I suddenly notice a strange sight. On the southward slope of the valley, at a distance of approximately 500 metres, up on the permanent snow, a being of unusual aspect is moving—reminiscent of a man's figure, but with a strongly hunched back. Against the white background it could be seen clearly that he was standing with his legs wide apart, and that his arms are longer than in the ordinary man. I stood there, not moving. And so five minutes elapse. The figure then vanished, hidden behind a rock.

"Three days later, returning from a reconnaissance, after sunset, I again saw that familiar figure, in that same valley. This time it was extremely brief, as the figure vanished into a dark depression, possibly a cave.

"A week later the people arrived, bringing their equipment. The place began to be noisy. The work of the expedition went ahead. The strange encounter was forgotten. But just before we left, our rubber boat suddenly vanished from the river bank, and our searches for it gave no results. We just had to lump it. It was only a month after we had left there that we received word, in Leningrad, that our colleagues of the scientific post of the Uzbek S.S.R's Academy of Science, who were operating not far from us, had found the boat five kilometres upstream from where we had lost it. It was fully intact. How could it have got up there? For, look you, to go up that boiling mountain torrent, abounding in rapids and shoals, would have been impossible in a boat.

"I must mention that I interrogated the local inhabitants— they were Kirghiz—and asked if they had seen a strange being, like a man, up on the rock faces. Some replied they had. They said that this being liked to be impudent. It had happened that some of them lost domestic utensils; troughs, basins, even clothing. And later on they found some of it away up on the heights. Are these facts not linked with the loss of our boat?

"You asked me why the talk of my meeting with a manlike being only came up in January, whereas it happened last August?

"Well, look, I am a hydrologist, and I have no intention of drawing conclusions in a sphere that is unknown to me. I had thought I would wait until there was a fresh expedition and then give my interest to this matter again. It is true that I had a talk with a Leningrad specialist in these matters, but it was also by way of mere speculation.

"People have said to me 'Why didn't you climb up there where the manlike creature was moving about and explore the depression where he secreted himself?' Such an opinion can only be expressed by folk who don't know the Pamirs. The shape was at a great altitude, on an absolutely sheer cliff face. Even an experienced alpinist would have found it difficult to get up there."

29

Abroad, this reasonably couched survey of what Pronin witnessed, was transmuted to a more colourful account of the creature who was alleged to have stared at Pronin at close quarters with deep sunken eyes—a physical impossibility in view of the distance between them. But as the account of the encounter took place in a conversation over the telephone, and probably with interpreters at both ends, misunderstandings in language can be excused.

It may be the language difficulty also that at the time of the garbled English version of the incident gave one the impression that Mr Pronin's adventure was receiving the mocking "oblivion" treatment Russian psychology is adept at applying at suitable moments.

CHAPTER FIVE

Relevant Russian Flash-backs

Though Doctor B. Porshnev at the time of the Pronin incident appeared to have been equally hushed up over the Snowman situation, from 1959 he must have been continuing his own investigations undeterred together with colleagues who like him had not closed the door on enquiries. There was continued watchfulness for developments, and re-examination on already acquired facts. That year the Doctor produced a series of surveys on "The Mystery of the Snowman". He asked:

"Does Nature, in the continent of Asia, and specifically Nature in the little explored high mountainous regions and uplands of Central Asia, perhaps still conceal a mystery that has remained unknown to world science down to our own days? Will perhaps one of the indirect results of the rapid progress being made by the peoples of Asia be the exposure of this mystery?

"Naturally, there are not a few sceptics who consider all the reports about the 'Snowman' to be fables. It is however true that today nobody any longer says that the Snowman was thought up by some particular individuals. For as soon as a start was made on gathering together interrogatory data, it became clear that the reports and accounts about this creature are spread across numerous peoples of the mountainous parts of Asia, even though they all give him different names. In translation most of these names mean 'Wild Man' or 'Man-Beast'.

"Science is faced with the choice of two decisions. The opponents who dispute the reality of the Snowman adduce the proposition that investigators have simply stumbled upon a

31

peculiar popular belief born of popular fantasy. They are inclined to be content with the view that such legends should be collected, written down, studied, but on one condition: namely that not biologists, but *folklorists* should occupy themselves with such matters.

"The protagonists for the Snowman's existence admit that they do not yet possess definite material proofs, that no living or dead Snowman has yet been secured, or even skeletal discoveries, and the whole question remains at the stage of the scientific hypothesis that is unprejudiced. Researchers with open minds suggest that in the present situation, (as in many others) science is the field where the hitherto sporadic investigations belong, and should continue.

"At the present time it is established that during the last few decades many people have seen the 'wild man' in the mountains of Asia. It is impossible to explain away those reports simply by popular beliefs alone. Among the witnesses were people who did not belong to the local population though familiar with local legends: geologists, travellers, sportsmen. In addition to this, large numbers of tracks have been found, left by this creature in the snow, or sometimes in sand. In many cases the cases were photographed or sketched, or plaster casts were taken from them. Zoologists established quite precisely that these belong neither to bear or monkey. But they are not human tracks either. Rather do they resemble the footprints of Man's prehistoric ancestors preserved in ancient caves.

"Science possesses descriptions of skins of the 'man-beast' secured at various times. Also records and photos of dried hands that seemed to have been cut off from dead specimens. And there are 'scalps' which, according to their owners, were taken from the heads of Snowmen."

It can be said here that the scalp claims as already indicated, were eventually dismissed in serious quarters. Regarding relics of alleged "dried hands", those too were probably not genuine. I remember in the fifties in the final stages of my previous research, seeing a privately shown colour film. This was a projection of stills taken of an alleged Yeti hand, mummified, but clearly defined. It had been taken on behalf of the late Tom Slick, a wealthy American oil man, and a passionately determined Yeti-chaser who spared no expense in his pursuit. In spite of his repeated attempts and expeditions in the Himalaya, his quarry eluded him. Like far more expert researchers and climbers, he found nothing in spite of his efforts and generous rewards for services. The "Yeti hand" was as false as the artefact scalps.

According to eye-witnesses of former years, people from time to time had managed to catch "wild men", stated Doctor Porshnev. They had even brought them into inhabited communities, but the captives soon died in the unaccustomed conditions. There were about ten of such cases on record; in 1912, 1914, 1937, 1941, and 1954, all in mountainous regions of the U.S.S.R. or China. Not a single skeleton or stuffed specimen of those caught was preserved.

The reason given now for this casual approach was that local officials or scholars at the time usually assumed that what they saw were just unique and solitary cases of abnormality or deformity of ordinary human beings. The thought never entered anybody's head that these were specimens of a special sort of creature, extremely rare, not a man in the strict sense of the word, but only "exceptionally" like a man in physical structure and appearance" to quote Doctor Porshnev again. The creature looked much nearer to man than the chimpanzee or gorilla. But all eye-witnesses reported that such beings showed no sign of articulated speech.

It was noticed, moreover, that the "Snowmen" possessed no working tools, that is, excluding stones or sticks, nor anything resembling clothing, and that their bodies were covered with hair.

The Porshnev surveys established that under the Tibetan name of "Mi-Gö", "Hün-Göröös" (Mongolian) or other terms, the ˉnowman was known from ancient times to contribute to Eastern medical prescriptions to cure certain ills, with particular reference to Tibetan folk-medicine. From the Snowman's fat, gall, and blood, medicinal concoctions were prepared. In old manuscript books on Medicine, among sketches depicting the human anatomy, there are representations of beings that were not in the least imaginary, but known to everybody. Living Asian animals, such as were encountered then and are encountered today. Among them appears the representation of the "*Mi-Gö*". Unlike the other purely animal creatures, he is shown standing on his two hind extremities.

Local folk knew in former days all about the *Almas*, or Yeti-Snowman; the majority of scholars and officials in the towns did not.

An ancient panel once on view in a Mongolian temple showed a circle of the animals of the regional mountains—the bear, the felines, the monkeys, and other beasts. Sitting cross-legged among them, obviously more human than the rest, squatted the "Hairy Man", gnomish, bristly, but not of recognised fauna species. I have seen a copy of it.

According to Doctor Porshnev, scientists may already have had in their possession important data warranting the assumption that in the mountains of Asia, and possibly in the Caucasus (as Professor Kofman's current field work is discovering) are survivors of the type of creature described, and for long unaccepted by Science. A highly organised primate, standing closer to Man than any other living being. The species may have held out only in areas still totally unsettled by Man, in the most inaccessible places and in the most unsuitable geographical conditions for civilised human habitation.

The species is clearly dying out rapidly, and in regions where encountered a few decades ago, today none is left. The most likely regions for the creature's habitat were suggested to be the savage mountainous areas of Sinkiang and Tibet.

And yet now researchers are faced with Professor Kofman's Caucasus discoveries. But these do tally with the Porshnev study of the whole question, and also with some of the views of other investigators in other parts of the world following their ov lines of enquiry independently.

"The term 'Snowman' must be taken to mean we are discussing some creature dwelling in the eternal snows," says

34

Doctor Porshnev. Many creatures have associated names, for instance, the "Snow Vulture", the "Snow Leopard", "Snow-Sheep". That last term is obviously the Russian name for the long-horned mountain sheep of Asia. The term "Snow" only signifies that any species to which it is attached belongs to fauna of the high mountains. The species may be seen on the snowfields when migrating (much like the Himalayan Snowman), but he lives and finds his food below the snowline among rocks and Alpine-type meadowlands, sometimes in sub-Alpine regions, or in the forests and zones of scrub growth on mountain slopes. The Alpine zones are characterised by rich vegetation and very varied fauna.

Local populations of the places the Doctor described reported that the Snowman fed on plants and roots, various insects, and also caught rodents, such as marmots and the Mouse-hare.

Probably like his Himalayan "cousin", the Snowman of the Russian mountain wildernesses might eat bodies of larger animals, but there some doubt should be cast, especially in view of Professor Kofman's Caucasus field work where she has deduced with her team that the local *Almas* appear to find a vegetarian diet more suited to their needs.

To judge from much earlier records, the Snowman fears mankind and flees from men. He is adapted for travelling across steep rock faces or snow-covered areas far better than is Man, or even than are hunting dogs. Nobody ever succeeded in catching him, apart from the very few cases of "wild men" being captured. There have been occasions when he has been trailed for forty-eight hours' at a stretch. The Snowman can observe the approach of man far sooner than man can detect him.

Local populations still say, and this is a current report, and based on Professor Kofman's work, that the Snowman, *Almas*, "Wild Man" possesses an inherent streak of curiosity. He is interested in, to him, unusual objects such as tents, personal effects, campfire sites, but he only approaches them under cover of darkness. There are good grounds for believing that he belongs in general to the category of nocturnal creatures, abroad at twilight and at dawn, and during night-time. They probably sleep

35

during the day.

There are very few accounts of people being attacked by Snowmen, and those stories that have been told were probably exaggerated. Not many scientists have ever at any time been inclined to accept as true what has been said about the "wild men". Not surprising, for so many accounts indicate fantasy and superstition, or the joke element. A large number of reports have been fictitious. An exaggerated image often attaches even to known animals or peoples. In some parts of the world supernatural qualities are attributed to bears. It follows that fables and legends can abound even more about the Snowman whose appearance is said to be so manlike.

"Scientists write off the superstitions," said Doctor Porshnev. "They mark on their maps the places where they are linked. There is good reason to believe that superstitions are widespread in those regions where that creature in olden days did actually exist, but where he has now died out." He added that nonetheless, a register of popular traditions could assist Science in solving the problem of the Snowman.

The Russian opinion is that until comparatively recently Western European and American investigators believed the Snowman was only found or spoken of on the southern slopes of the Himalaya and adjacent mountain ranges. In spite of the collected reports so long ago of Prjevalsky about the "Man-Beast" disproving this. The Russian and Mongolian scientists, Baradyn, Khakhlov, Jamtsarano, Simukov, and Rinchen, went on maintaining on the basis of their own extensive data that such a creature existed in several desert regions of Mongolia, and in North-West China.

The "Man-Beast", they believed, was still to be found only a few years ago, still in all the vast tracts of mountainous Asia, from the Himalaya in the south to the Altai Mountains and the Gobi Desert in the north. At the time when they reached their deductions, they called upon Chinese scientists to partake in the study of the problem. Relations between Russia and China being in better shape a few years ago than now in the sixties, some valuable reports stemmed from their co-operation.

36

The Russians through that co-operation and associated work, were able to construct a chart showing the Snowman distribution. To judge by that map of a few years ago, if their suppositions were correct, the creature's habitat zone was steadily contracting throughout the period covered by History. It must be still shrinking with the passage of years.

And yet, Professor Kofman's field work in the Caucasus suggests by her down-to-earth eye-witnesses' reports, and the careful evidence of her own team, that the *Almas*, Snowman, Yeti, "wild man" is there, and is neither legend, hallucination, nor *Shaitan*.

CHAPTER SIX

More Russian Records

Other flash-backs of importance were dealt with in a September 1959 survey by Doctor Porshnev.

In assembling information of facts spread over many years and collected from several sources, there is bound to be some duplication. This occurs because information is based from different persons' discoveries and viewpoints, but for clarity they must be given, while treating them as succintly as possible.

First comes the question of the Russian "blueprint" chart of Snowman distribution. At the time of its preparation area chartings were up-to-date. Now they are not, in view of revelations in the Caucasian field work. But the experts of those few years ago correctly noted much of the fauna distribution, and were able to associate the presence of Snowmen or *Almas* with the presence of certain fauna in a specified area.

They discovered that Snowman and Snow Leopard distributions were located in the same areas. There was serious ground for relating their location to the same altitudes, they said. There was also ground for suggesting that both these species were formed and developed in the same period of the earth's history, and that they were close biological neighbours. This seems difficult to accept, or quite understand. One wonders whether this allegedly biological link might have been formulated from repeated and doubtful allegations that in some high altitudes the tracks of so-called Snowmen are really the tracks of snow leopard?

There is much room for confusion and straying too far from possibilities in fringe regions of research.

An interesting popular Russian theory was based on the fact that the snow leopard, unlike the ordinary leopard, never attacks

38

man, even when wounded. This instinct might have developed in the Snow Leopard during a course of long-drawn-out natural selection, implying that the animal never developed aggressiveness towards man because generations of the species were accustomed to a non-attacking Snowman in the vicinity. One might add to this that the presence of the Snowman may have served as a deterrent to civilised man's settlement in such regions. Consequently, the Snow Leopard was seldom hunted by man, and consequently it never attacked the nearest approach to man—the Snowman.

The fact of Snowman and Snow Leopard as neighbours in such wild regions could give the clue to another problem that occupies the naturalist. People in Russia often ask: "Why does nobody find Snowman carcases, or even their bones?" It was then possible to counter this with another question: "And why does nobody ever find, under natural conditions, bones or carcases of the Snow Leopard? Why is it that even *fossilized* bones of snow leopard have never been found?" The experts gave simple reasons for this, says Doctor Porshnev. The carcases were dragged away by predators, and bones get washed away and broken up by mountain torrents.

Outside questioners often ask why nothing has been heard about the Snowman until comparatively recent years, if it was true that the species lived, unidentified, in vast tracts of mountainous Asia? Surely, they argue, past peoples must have come across him and among them there must have been students of the mystery?

Past and present people including scientists, have faced this problem repeatedly. Tackling the question at closer quarters, it was soon established by modern researchers that they were dealing with a creature that long ago did attract the attention of mankind, and whose image has often appeared in man's folklore.

Evidence of the Snowman appears, it must be repeated, in the *Ramayana* written by Sri Valmiki of the third or fourth century B.C. There is also relevant reference in an ancient Babylonian piece of writing, "Poem of Gilgamish". This belongs to the third millenium B.C. References are found in the records of other

39

writers of antiquity, like Pliny; in a Kirghiz epic poem, "Manas", and in books of early European travellers who went to Asia, and other remote parts of the earth. A certain writer, one Kircher, visited South China in the seventeenth century. He was reported to have published a travel book in Amsterdam, in which he gave evidence of "Wild men" living in China and Northern India. Kircher's evidence may have served as basis for the great eighteenth century Swedish naturalist, Karl Linnaeus, to include specifications of the Snowman or "Wild Men" when he produced his classifications of animals.

The term "Manas" is interesting, for it occurred also in a region far from the land of the Kirghiz. This was in Northern India. During her work at high altitudes in 1950 Mira Behn questioned herdsmen concerning a report she had heard. A group of herdsmen had pursued and killed a so-called Snowman who had kidnapped one of their women. They told Mira Behn that they had not reported the incident to the authorities because they were afraid of being charged with murder. They looked upon "The Hairy Man" as a human being. The local name for these creatures was Van Manas. They were at times seen raiding plantations, and their tracks were often found in the snow or even on soft ground on lower slopes where cultivation of food attracted them. The local people accepted those occasional incursions as merely of nuisance character.

The distance between the near-Mongolian land of the Kirghiz and the mountain communities of Northern India is roughly 2,300 miles. Names have a mysterious way of circling the world, and often such names denote the same thing. Those two geographical Snowmen or Yeti points of interest and similarity, situated at wide intervals appear on my imaginary S Map of Snowman distribution, and it was prepared and published before any knowledge of the Russian chart.

The Russians suggested there had been sporadic pre-scientific knowledge about the Snowman. They have also kept records of their own first successes and mishaps in that field, where they operated under frequently difficult conditions.

In the years 1905/1907, a young scientist and oriental student,

B. B. Baradiyn, of Buriat-Mongolian nationality, was engaged by the Russian Geographical Society of those days to undertake a mission across Mongolia to Tibet. Subsequently, he told a great friend of his, Scientist Mongolian expert, Ts. Zh. Jamtsarano, of his experiences while his caravan was crossing the Alashan Desert. Russian reports place this in a region known as the Badyn-Dzharan Tract.

One evening just before sundown, Baradiyn's caravan leader gave a yell and pointed to a strange figure clambering up a sand dune. The whole party could see clearly the head of what seemed to be a long-haired man resembling an ape. For some time it stood bending and reaching downwards with long arms. It then hid behind the crest of the dune.

Baradiyn' party included a very sturdy and athletic lama from the district of Urga. His name was Shirab Siplyy, and he was renowned for his physical prowess. Now he set off in pursuit of the Almas (as the Mongols had always called the species.) The lama did not succeed in spite of his remarkable speed, and Baradiyn had no camera.

On his return to St Petersburg, as the Russian capital was then called, he produced a written report of the surprising encounter. But when his paper was about to be printed he ran into the same official difficulties that had faced Prjevalsky years before. Baradiyn's science chief, S. F. Oldenburg, an Academician, and Permanent Secretary of the Russian Academy of Sciences, ordered him to erase from his report any account of the occurrence. Once again, the fear of social embarrassment hushed up an interesting incident.

Throughout his whole life B. B. Baradiyn never had a chance to publish his findings. However, inspired by his description, Ts. Zh. Jamtsarano and his assistants, Geographer A. D. Simukov, and the Mongologist, Dr Rinchen (who is still alive) continued for many years to study in Mongolia the problem of Almas' existence. Mr Simukov took part in an expedition the Russians referred to as "The P. K. Kozlov" expedition. (Kozlov was a great explorer of Central Asia, on a par with Prjevalsky in reputation.)

Doctor Rinchen's pursuit of the *Almas* riddle earned a certain amount of success, probably more so within the Russian borders than in the West. Even years later in 1968 the West had little opportunity to examine the question.

There was a barrage of non-cooperation and official apathy in most countries.

Just after Baradiyn had met the *Almas*, V. A. Khakhlov, a young zoologist, took a trip in 1907 up the glaciers known as the Ala-Tau, part of the Saur and Tarbagatay glaciers. He heard from his Kazakh guide for the first time in his life about the existence of "Wild men" in the region of Dzungaria. Then, in 1910 he was told that in the Pamirs the local population spoke of a similar creature inhabiting regions to the East of the Pamirs.

Khakhlov mentioned the reports to his chiefs at the Moscow University. These were a future Academician called Menzbir, and one P. P. Sushkin. The first totally rejected the possibility of wild men existing, but Sushkin advised him to go on collecting data, observing that travellers in Central Asia had in fact also heard of the presence of wild men in those parts, and P. K. Kozlov the famous Russian explorer, in particular had, it seems, already spoken to Sushkin about this.

Khakhlov abandoned his University work for a while, and turned explorer. He spent two or three years travelling in the regions of Dzungaria, adjoining the Zaysan and Tarbagatay mountain ranges. He listened to all the evidence, writing down everything that in any way related to the wild men. What interested him first and foremost was the fact that every time he tried to pinpoint the region where this creature dwelt, he ran up against the almost unvarying answer: "It's away over there, far away where there are wild horses, and wild camels."

One Kirghiz name for wild horse is *at-gyik*; for wild camels, *t'ë-gyik*; for wild men, *ksy-gyik*. Khakhlov in his piecemeal but concentrated research, could not help associating those three together as creatures distributed in very similar geographical terrain.

At last he found two witnesses among Kazakh tribesmen who had seen a "wild man" in Central Asia where their Kazakh kinsmen lived. Each of these men had seen their wild men at different places, and neither witness knew anything about the other. The young zoologist put them through separate and detailed interrogation, and this yielded valuable and convincing scientific results.

A year before that interrogation, one of the two Kazakhs had been in the Iren'-Kabyrga Mountains with a local herdsman. They were pasturing their horses by night and at dawn they saw what they thought was a man. Suspecting him to be a horse thief they quickly jumped into the saddle and with their long herds-men's sticks with horse-hair lassoes, set after him. The "man" ran awkwardly and not very fast, and they soon put two lassoes around him. As they caught him, he cried, or rather, he squeaked —"just like a hare". Looking closely at their prisoner, the local Kazakh herdsman explained to the visiting Kazakh that this was a "wild man"—an inoffensive creature that never harmed people, and that they should let him go.

The species was a male, of less than medium human height, and covered with hair, "just like a young camel," said the local herdsman. [The Central Asian dromedary of Mongolia and China with two humps, has thick reddish winter fur, rather like a teddy bear.] But what was really striking about the captive was his long arms, reaching to below the knees. He was stooped, with shoulders bent forward, and had a narrow, hollow chest. His brow was sloping, and the brows jutted out sharply above the eyes. His lower jaw was massive, and he was chin-less, the nose small, with big nostrils. He had large ears with no lobes, and somewhat pointed towards the rear, "Just like a fox's". The skin on his forehead, forearms, and knees was horny and calloused, his legs far apart and bent at the knees. The soles of his feet resembled human feet, but were one and a half times or twice as broad, with widely set toes. The big toe was shorter than in a man's, and set apart from the other toes. The hands, with their long fingers, had some resemblance to a man's. A curious feature was that he had a protuberance at the back of the neck, rather like some dogs have.

When, on the insistence of the Kazakh herdsman, the wild

43

man was set free, the two followed him and discovered his hide-out. It was a hollowed-out spot beneath an overhanging cliff, into which a lot of long dried grass had been thrown. Afterwards the local people told the Kazakh herdsman who was relating this story, of a whole series of additional reports about the creature. The species, they said, lived generally in pairs, were only rarely seen, and were harmless to humans.

Another witness whom V. A. Khaklov found, had observed a "wild man" specimen over a period of several months near the Manas River. That specimen, a female, had been caught and made captive by local farmers. The creature had been chained to a small mill, until finally set at liberty. The "wild woman" answered to previous descriptions of the *Almas*. Her body was covered with hair, she was narrow-chested and stooping, with inordinately long arms, widely set legs, and large flat feet with spreading toes. The foot was very broad, and looked like a paw.

She emitted sounds only occasionally, but bared her teeth when anybody came near her during her captivity, and when she slept it was in a peculiar position—like a camel, the narrator said, with knees and elbows underneath her, forehead touching the ground, and hands at the back of her neck. Of food offered her, she only ate raw meat, a few kinds of greenstuff, and grain. Later, though, she refused meat and developed a taste for flat loaves of bread. Sometimes she seized and devoured insects that came within her reach. She drank either by lying prostrate to the water and drinking "like a horse", or by dripping water into her mouth with her hand. When she was set at liberty, she walked off clumsily, long arms dangling, and then ran and hid in the nearby swamps.

Such were the accounts V. A. Khakhlov obtained from two Kazakh herdsmen who became his companions and guides at different times in his exploration. He translated their reports into the language of contemporary science. What he had learnt aston-ished him. He decided that the declarants would have been in-capable of inventing such stories, and had they done so, the imaginations of two different men could not have been in almost total agreement. These were two witnesses entirely unknown to each other, and who knew nothing of zoology or anthropology.

By way of an additional check, Khakhlov had photographed illustrations that showed a gibbon, a chimpanzee, a gorilla, and a reconstructed sketch of Prehistoric Man. He showed the photographs to each witness at different times, with a request that they should indicate which of the photos most resembled the "Wild men" species. Both men pointed to the picture of Prehistoric Man.

V. A. Khakhlov on his return from his research, told P. P. Sushkin of his discoveries, and his encounters with the two Kazakh witnesses. He received encouragement from him and at the same time Khakhlov set about preparing a new expedition; a small one to go to Sinkiang with the view to securing and sending back to Russia either heads, hands, or feet of "wild men" so that an anatomical determination of the unknown species might be made.

Again obstacles made this an abortive effort. The killing of a creature resembling man externally, and the despatch of the remains across the Russo-Chinese frontier would have caused too much trouble, suspicion, and landed him into legal difficulties, to say the least of it. Khakhlov consequently decided to request official support of the Russian Academy of Sciences. The request was sent off. Months of vexatious waiting elapsed, and silence reigned. Finally, the young zoologist learned indirectly that it had been decided to "take no action" on his request. That was in 1914. The first world war then broke out. In 1915 he had to return to Moscow University.

There must have been a long interruption to any more research on the Snowman, or unknown species, for a gap of years seems to have followed. As far as interested enquirers know, nothing intensive in research seems to have been carried out during that time, and in view of the world's history, that would not be surprising. Snowman and *Almas* questions must have been shelved or dismissed, and even if sporadic reports circulated, they were not important compared with world affairs.

In the spring of 1959, Doctor Boris Porshnev learned in common with others who had always been interested in the unsolved

problem, that V. A. Khakhlov was still interested in the Snowman.

Khakhlov had by then developed into a white-haired honoured
savant, a Professor of Comparative Animal Anatomy who had
during his many years enriched the science of zoology with valuable and original contributions.

Those ten years ago he spoke, during an interview, of his
research, and he talked with animation and bitterness about his
discoveries on the very threshold of which he had stood in the
days of his youth, and which had only decades later been introduced into the agenda of World Science. What embittered him
was not merely apathy of leadership in the Academy of Science
of pre-revolution days. In 1928, Academician P. P. Sushkin had
propounded a bold hypothesis that startled the whole scientific
world, he said. This was a theory that the original homeland of
Man, the region where the transformation from ape to man took
place, was in the high mountain region of Asia. In a book he
wrote on the subject, Sushkin used this hypothesis to make a
number of deductions, but he said not one solitary word about
the very relevant reports on the "wild man" species of Central
Asia that had once been given to him by V. A. Khakhlov and
P. K. Kozlov.

It is not merely the authority of "official Science" that has
long been an impediment to the unravelling of the Snowman or
Almas enigma. The main obstacle has been, according to Russian
opinion, the scattered and disjointed nature of the data possessed
by individual observers and investigators working in the various
regions of Asia and elsewhere. This factor operates as an obstacle
not only in Asia but in every place on earth where the enigma
appears and re-appears sporadically.

Researchers everywhere have had the same problems linked
with the same unintentional ignorance. Running into one or
other of the reports about the mysterious creature in some particular region, they never suspected that exactly the same kind
of reports existed in respect of other regions. They were not in
possession of the necessary material so that they might make a
correlation. They were unable to employ the test of comparison,

46

Science's basic instrument. As the result of this lack of communication many studies were fruitless and came to nought.

Here is an example: Some years ago, still in Russia, a geologist, B. M. Zdorik, wrote that to his great regret, when he was working in the Pamirs in 1926/1938, he had never heard a thing, even as late as that decade, about the Himalayan Snowman (the Yeti). Consequently he was unable to grasp what the people in the Pamirs were talking about when they told him about the "shaggy wild men" there, some of whom he had glimpsed himself.

Other similar experiences of his took place when he was working in 1929 in a range of mountains known as the Sanglakh, a westerly spur of Peter the First Range. When questioning the local population about the fauna of the district he was given an interesting but non-sensational list by the chairman of the Tutkaul Soviet. This included wild boar, bear, red wolf, hyena, porcupine and jackal. Then the geologist was amazed to learn another name, *Deva*, or *Dev*. Some people in certain other regions had at times used the name to describe an "unclean spirit". Here it was treated as part of the fauna along with the wolf and other specified animals.

There is a connotation here with the Snowman situation away in Bhutan, and this will be amplified in a later chapter.

The headman of the locality where Zdorik was operating told him that the *Dev* resembled a small, very thickset man, that it walked on two legs, and had a head and body covered with brown hair. Other now familiar details followed. According to this headman the *Dev* was encountered extremely rarely in the Sanglakh Mountains, but turned up now and again either alone or in pairs. He had never seen any young ones, but during the previous summer (remember, this was in 1929, and what the position is now in the late 60's is so far unknown) the Tadjiks, a local tribe, had caught a grown one alive at a mill where it had been regaling itself with flour and grain. This had taken place on the eastern slopes of the mountain ridge, only a few kilometres from Tutkaul.

They kept the captive *Dev* chained up for two months, feeding

47

it (or him) with raw meat and flatcakes of barley flour. Eventually, the lucky *Dev* broke his chain and escaped. Villagers showed Zdorik a man whose head showed a big scar said to be from a wound inflicted on him by a *Dev*.

In 1934 B. M. Zdorik himself encountered one of these creatures. He was making his way with a Tadjik guide, along a network of paths running through thickets of wild alpine *grechika*. This usually means buckwheat, but in this context must mean some sort of rough shrub. They were standing on a small almost inaccessible mountain plateau lying at about 2500/2800 metres above sea level between the Darvaz Range and the westerly spur of the Peter The First Range. In his report, Zdorik wrote: "Suddenly, a small area opened up in front of us on which the grass was completely flattened, and the ground dug up as if it had been done with a spade. On the path were drops of blood and scraps of what looked like marmot fur. But there, right at my very feet, on a heap of freshly dug earth, an unknown creature lay asleep. It was lying fully stretched out on its stomach, about 1½ metres or so in length. I could not see the head and front limbs very well as they were hidden from me by a withered *grechika* bush. I did manage to see the legs and the bare black feet which were too long and too well shaped to be a bear's. The whole body of the animal was covered with shaggy hair looking more like yak's wool than the downy pelt of a bear. The hair colour was reddish-brown, redder than I have ever seen on a bear. The creature's flanks rose and fell rhythmically as it slept. I stood there frozen with surprise, and at a loss as to what to do. I looked back at my Tadjik guide who was following close behind me. He was standing there stupified, his face as white as a sheet. Then with a gesture he pulled me silently by the sleeve and indicated to me that I must run at once.

"Never before, had I seen such an expression of terror on a man's face. His fear communicated itself to me, and beside ourselves, without glancing backwards at the creature, we both fled away down the path, enmeshing ourselves and stumbling about in the high grass."

On the following day Zdorik learned from the local people

that they were extremely interested, but alarmed by this encounter. What he had stumbled upon was a sleeping *Dev*, they said. At the time he recorded this happening, he jotted down too that the Tadjiks used some other name for the animal, if animal it was. It occurred to him as he re-examined the whole situation that the local inhabitants were only calling the mystery creature a *Dev* so that he having heard the term before would now understand better what they were saying.

According to the people of somewhat nearby Tal'bar and Saffeder valleys, there were quite a few families of those *Devs*, males, females, and young, living in the mountains. The creatures were considered to be of the animal kingdom, and not the supernatural agencies of unclean powers, as some believed. Neither man nor domestic animal was ever harmed by them. But to meet them, ah, that was another matter. The *Dev* was *thought* to be an evil omen.

Before his experience in those mountainous parts, so isolated from civilisation, Zdorik had never believed the local tales about the existence of wild manlike creatures. That was long before his encounter with the sleeping *Dev*.

The name varies, but the problem remains.

Carl Linneaus in the eighteenth century, gave the name *Homo Nocturnus* (that is "Night Man") to the much debated species. V. A. Khakhlov in the twentieth century had suggested the title *Primihomo Asiaticus*, (First Asian Man). In 1955/58, the Belgian zoologist, Bernard Heuvelmans, based his theories almost exclusively on data from the Himalaya, apparently knowing nothing as yet of the above two suggestions. He performed another christening with the name *Dinantropoides Nivalis*, meaning *Abominable Snow Anthropoid*.

In established zoology, experts adhere to a firm custom: a newly discovered species is officially given the name that is first suggested. This is entirely ruled by convention, and regardless of whether that first name is harmonious or descriptive. In cases of necessity only the generic name, that is, the first word in the title can be changed. There is probably a good reason for this rigidity in that it would avoid confusion in identification, reference, and

49

study in the years to come. In view of the confusion and argument that occurs over any hotly contested question, one wonders that it has ever worked. Nature generally has the last word, and turns the tables on many of the experts, sometimes after hundreds of years.

It is still too early to make an issue over this curious naming, not "of parts", but of officially unknown creatures.

The scientist P. P. Pavlov once said: "Science is supported by facts as a bird's wing is supported by air."

CHAPTER SEVEN

Mongolian Candidates

Many of the factors presented in earlier chapters receive associated confirmation in this one. The jigsaw-puzzle pieces dovetail as if drawn together magnetically across a large surface of the globe.

Because of the range of research in which records like this one involve authors, someone once humorously referred to me as "reaching to Outer Mongolia". Prophetic words perhaps dropped in casual talk. In October 1968 I had to write to Professor Doctor Rinchen, eminent Mongolian scientist whom I have quoted earlier. After the passage of months I got his answer to my asking him for more news, if such information was in his power to impart. In spite of his continuous professional commitments he found time to reply, and he sent me copies of deductions he had prepared, and which had been used for his numerous reports and lectures.

Delays caused by slowness in communications were now clearing up, and the policy of patience was bringing results. Not being patient by nature, but by the nature of my work, this was to me specially rewarding.

Professor Rinchen told how in recent years the "so-called Snowman" (his term) had evoked the attention of countries in the West. How, while some readers and investigators are inclined to think that the Snowman really does exist as an excessively rare species still inhabiting the unpopulated tracts of Asia, others are convinced that we must treat belief in his existence as we treat tales of fairies and gnomes. What then, enquired Professor Rinchen, of the numerous reports from travellers, frontier guards, and all those who have encountered this mysterious being. Hallucinations? Encounters with phantoms in the Gobi

Desert and the Himalaya?

That other famous professor, the late Doctor Jamtsarano, comes into the picture again here. He was a lifelong and well-known expert on Mongolian, and founder of the Mongolia Academy of Science which was described by Professor Rinchen as "the highest scientific institution in our country".

Jamtsarano was convinced that in the vast uninhabited expanse of the great Gobi Desert there existed, unknown to Science, the wild man the Mongols knew, and still know as the *Almas*. But he was convinced too that the few reports of the existence of the *Almas* carried little power of conviction for official science. It was necessary to produce addition to mere reports. Evidence that in his time Prjevalsky produced for Science when he brought back sketches he had made in the deserts of Mongolia, of the wild horse known today as *Prjevalsky's Horse*. The Mongols, said the professor, had known from times immemorial of this wild horse's existence, had hunted him, eaten his flesh, and used his hide for household purposes. Professor Rinchen said that, but for the ambitious drive of the Russian explorer who had discovered the animal and drawn the attention of Europeans to the fact, the learned world of western savants would have followed the tradition of disregarding "native" names for animals and plants.

The Mongol name for their wild horse is *tahi*. Among the fields of established knowledge of those days a local name was sufficient to relegate its possessor to the realms of folk tradition and fable. The *tahi* definitely exists, though it is very nearly extinct.

The same premise can apply to the *Almas*. In his wild horse discovery, Prjevalsky had brought back, apart from his sketch, the skeleton and hide of the *tahi* he had stumbled upon in his research, but he had not been so lucky in *Almas* reports. Professor Jamtsarano had not been lucky in the *Almas* investigation either, though in his time he had been one of the first to try and tackle the *Almas* problem. As in the case of Prjevalsky's *Almas* reports, it was not his fault that he did not succeed in carrying out his investigations to their conclusion.

Successive bodies of authority appear to have played down the living riddle of the Snowman or "Hairy People". And yet many peoples of Asia, Mongols, Tibetans, Kirghiz, Kazakhs, Nepalese, and others, knew of the existence of a creature that could be described as Man's kinsman. And down the centuries records can be found of individuals whose curiosity and interest were aroused by stories relating to this creature.

Plano Carpini was a monk whom Pope Innocent IV, in the thirteenth century, sent to Mongolia to act as his first ambassador to that country. Carpini learned during his term of office about the "Wild People" of those ancient times. They were found southwards from the town of Hanyl, once built by the Emperor Ogotay. That town, one of the three main cities of Sinkiang, is known to present-day Mongols as Hamil, though in modern parlance it is called Hami.

To the investigating Russians of recent decades it was significant that the Gobi Desert Mongols still considered the hairy bi-pedal "wild men" of those vast regions, as men of a kind, and not actual animals, and certainly not supernatural entities, incorporate souls, with which some human imaginings peopled immense wildernesses.

Nomads of those regions noted that the Almas, like the wild horse, and the wild camel, fled from close propinquity with man. They gradually withdrew as the nomads brought more pasture land into practical use.

The Hairy creatures' distribution seems to have been a subject that induced different persons to draw maps presenting such distribution, and Doctor Jamtsarano was one of these. In his map he concentrated on the Gobi region, and marked on it all the spots where caravaneers, wandering monks, lama-monks, nomad herdsmen, princes, officials, hunters and messengers had all seen the strange beings or noticed their tracks. Professor Rinchen said: "On that map, basing facts on oral reports, we outlined the zone of putative Almas habitation from the close of the nineteenth century up to 1928."

The map showed how the areas of habitation were shrinking more and more, and were moving from east to west. A remarkable thing also shown on his and his colleagues' map was that the wild horse (*tahi*) and the wild camel (called in Mongolian, *havtgay*) were moving westward too.

An artist called Soeltay who worked at the Academy of Sciences on Doctor Jamtsarano' material, painted pictures of the *Almas*, and then had informants add their corrections. On the final approved sketches Doctor Jamtsarano noted: "*Almas*, according to so-and-so".

The drift westward might have some relation to the current *Almas* discoveries by Professor Kofman in the Caucasus, and this migration from Mongolian wilds to perhaps, for them, more fruitful valleys and uplands might account for the wide spread of evidence she and her team collected, and are still collecting.

Almas in Doctor Jamtsarano's day answered to much the same descriptions as those the Kofman team assembled. The *Almas* of Mongolia too were very similar to men, they wore no clothes and were covered with reddish-black hair. This was not at all thick like that found among the large animals of the Gobi, for skin could be seen between the hairs. They walked, said the older records, with knees half bent and with a stooping gait. Their jaws were powerful, and brows low with jutting ridges above the eyes. The female *Almas* had long breasts. While seated on the ground, stated one informant, they could toss the breasts over their shoulders to feed their young which stood or crouched behind their mothers. That custom, however, has been known to be prevalent among actual recognised tribes in other parts of the world.

The Mongols of the Gobi Desert have always been excellent trackers. They would observe that the *Almas* tracks were set more "edgewise" than human footprints. That is probably due to the fact that the *Almas* stride causes the main body weight to fall on the outer edge of the foot. The Mongols used to call them *Habisun mörtu*, which in the Mongol tongue means "edgewise-going". A saying of theirs on record is "As shaggy as an *Almas*" when they wanted to describe a very unkempt wild-looking person. With them the *Almas* had the reputation of being ugly and maladorous, male and female alike. Aged old females of the species were called "Old Saxaul women." These creatures lived a sort of outcast life among the thickets of saxaul bushes.

Use of fire or of weapons was always unknown to the *Almas*. This may still be so among whatever shrinking distribution of them may exist. They never had any habitation as we know it.

During his lifetime Doctor Jamtsarano and his informants related to Professor Rinchen many curious cases of meetings between the Gobi people and the *Almas*. In 1927 a caravan was left unattended while the occupants went back a short distance to trace a camel that had dropped out. When they came back at daybreak they encountered several *Almas* who were warming themselves at the dying camp fire. It did not occur to them to keep it alight by throwing on some saxaul branches from nearby bushes. They had eaten all the dried dates and sweets the leading caravaneer had been bringing back for his children, but had left jars of Chinese wine untouched.

In the summer of 1928 Doctor Rinchen himself halted overnight at the home of an old Mongol woman of the Gobi. She was well in her seventies. She told him how once a female *Almas* had nursed her at the breast. Her father had gone to Sinkiang with a caravan and her mother had gone to the well to water a herd of sheep, leaving her baby unattended in the yurt; a felt-covered nomad tent still used by these nomads. Returning with the sheep the mother suddenly heard her child crying, and noticed that the felt cover of the entrance to the yurt was thrown back. The alarmed mother rushed in and saw a hideous naked woman, her body covered with sparse reddish hair, sitting on the women's side (east) of the yurt beside the small Mongolian crib, and putting one of her long breasts into the child's mouth. The mother cried in horror and flung herself across the yurt to protect her child. The hairy creature gave a start as she heard her scream, quickly put the child down, and, leaping past the mother, ran out.

The woman had noticed that the strange creature was pigeon-toed, and her feet were bleeding. A fleeting sighting as she hobbled away, showed her with arms longer than human arms that dangled by her sides. She disappeared into a grove of saxaul trees.

Later on the Mongol mother learnt that the creature was thought to have been a female *Almas* that had probably lost a child of her own, and whose breasts were over-full of milk.

Professor Rinchen's old lady hostess concluded this account of her childhood experience with the words: "I have never been ill in my life. The old folk used to say this was because I had drunk of *Almas* milk."

The Professor told how in 1930 he met a Kazakh in Ulaanbaatar, the capital city of Mongolia, who had come from the Soviet Union to teach in the Gobi-Altay area. Professor Rinchen could not remember his name, but the man told him of an incident that I too had heard, and had quoted in my previous Snowman book. This was how a Kazakh community in the Gobi had once seen the body of a young *Almas* girl. She had been killed accidentally when she touched a cross-bow wire set as a trap to snare wild animals. The sparsely populated community were fully aware of the accident to the *Almas* child, who was about seven years old. They begged of enquirers "Please don't tell anybody about this, because cross-bow snares are now illegal." This incident is similar to the *Van Manas* killing in the Himalaya when the tribesmen who had rescued their kinswoman from a "Hairy Man" and killed him, did not dare report the happening for fear they might be charged with murder.

The Professor's informant of the death of the child *Almas* told also how at the beginning of that same year he was out hunting with local Kazakhs, and at sundown in a snowdrift met a completely naked man who ran off at the sight of them, despite their shouts to stop him. He was hairy and went charging through the deep snow waving his arms about. One of the Kazakhs, the teacher, wanted to shoot at the creature, but companions prevented him, saying that to kill an "*Almast*", as the Kazakhs called the *Almas*, could bring on bad weather, more snow, and dearth of fodder! Nonetheless the teacher, feeling more enlightened, mounted his horse and went after the fugitive, but the horse floundered in deep snow, and the naked hairy creature vanished. In describing the occurrence afterwards, the Russian Kazakh teacher said: "I was blinded by the sun, but I saw the

Doctor K. Ramamurti (without hat) and a colleague crossing a rope bridge on one of his trips while modernising the postal service of Bhutan. (Photo taken on Chazam Bridge— Tashigang, Bhutan)

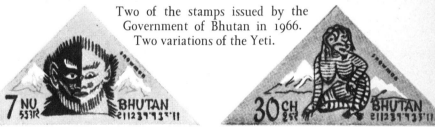

Two of the stamps issued by the Government of Bhutan in 1966. Two variations of the Yeti.

Wienczyslaw Plawinski examining the skull that he was to later reconstruct.

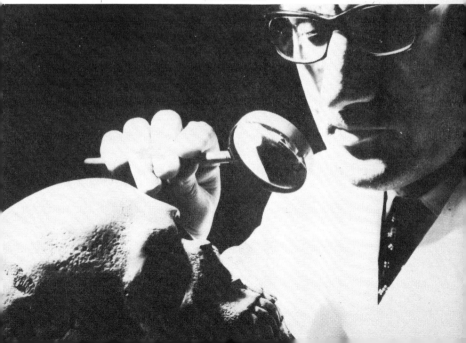

Novosti Press Agency (A.P.N.)

Above, Professor B. Porshnev.

Professor Rinchen, on the right, with W. Plawinski on a visit to Poland in 1967.

fellow at a distance of about 100 metres. His body hair shone red in the evening sunlight. Persuade the adviser of your Ministry of Education to send someone out there to catch an *Almas!* Or organise an expedition by the Science Committee. I'll take part in it, and I'll show you the place where I saw the body of the *Almas* girl."

But committees react in a curiously apathetic way the world over.

In one of his reports Professor Rinchen commented with some irony: "In all those years I would have had more hope of shooting an arrow into Interplanetary Space than of trying to find any support from anybody among the advisers for an expedition to the Gobi to look for the remains of a little girl *Almas* that had run into a game-trap!"

Some Mongolian soldiers in 1940 told him how they shot some *Almas* on the South-West frontier between Mongolia and China. In the pre-dawn darkness they had mistaken them for saboteurs. But they were not contrite at all at having mistaken the *Almas* for human vandals. To them they were just wild animals.

Innumerable more witnesses of *Almas* encounters spoke to Professor Rinchen, or passed on information. A lame monk, one Dambayorin, was travelling across the Gobi in 1930, and seeing a naked child one evening, thought it had strayed and was lost. On coming near he saw its body was covered with red hair and realising here was an *Almas* child, he fled in terror. Many lamas believed the *Almas* were unclean beings that possessed magical powers of sorcery. Round about that same period a Mongol herds-woman also took to her heels on meeting a naked *Almas* child.

People said it was an ill omen to meet an *Almas* in a lonely place. There were several encounters during those years in the thirties. Once a herdsman driving a herd of horses one night, was attacked by a female *Almas* but managed to beat her off. But normally they were reputed, among the more informed people, to be harmless.

Certain of those confrontations had a humorous twist, as in the case of Herdsman Gotop. He was attacked by an *Almas* at night in the Öndör Höhö Uul (The High Blue Mountains). He

57

only managed to shake off his assailant by slipping out of his high felt boots and throwing them at the *Almas* whose interest was thus diverted.

An archaeologist, named Dordjisurum, of the Historical Institute of the Science Committee, told the Professor in recent years, that at the end of 1930's, one very bad winter, in his native region of North-West Mongolia, a hairy man took refuge in a nomad camp. The dogs drove him off, and the women were relieved, for their particular folklore tradition specified this *Almas* as being a man-eater. There was famine that year and several wild animals had been driven by hunger to raid the camps. Probably lack of food had forced that *Almas* also to enter that belt of near-civilisation.

Different localities seemed to have acquired their own *Almas*-tradition.

In 1958, the manager of a chemist's shop in Ulaanbaatar, called Nagmit, told Professor Rinchen how amazed he himself had been, when he met an *Almas*, at the strength of the creature's biceps and leg muscles, and the heavy hair on back and chest which was shorter than on the head where it was long and grey. Nagmit was in wild mountain territory on that occasion, with two local Kazakhs, and a local schoolmaster. They shouted to the *Almas*, offering clothes and food, but the wild man kept a prudent distance. When they tried to shoot low at the "safe" part of his legs, the creature seemed merely curious, and then made off. The local Kazakhs were angry at the shooting even if it had been done just to arrest the *Almas* on the spot and not injure him seriously. These Kazakhs looked upon their own particular brand of *Almas* as rulers of the mountains and they were annoyed that visitors should take the liberty of trying to shoot at one.

This story, one of the many samples of data Professor Rinchen received caused a good deal of attention when the report appeared in one of the numbers of *Sovremennaya Mongoliya* (*Contemporary Mongolia*). It had been unfortunate that Nagmit had had no camera with him during his mountain trip, so as to record the incident. That goes too for most of the other records of similar meetings.

An old friend of the Professor called Gopil told him of *Almas*-tracking in wild saxaul-bush country, when mounted on camels, travellers tried to capture "specimens". Even fleet-footed camels failed to catch up with them. On approach, especially in the case of the old and shaggy females, they would utter such blood-chilling shrieks that the pursuing camels would take fright and back away in terror.

Gopil also told of a kidnapping that took place in the Gobi. A caravan was travelling to the town of Höhö Hot in Inner Mongolia, and they halted in the Gobi. One of the party went off to collect the camels that had been let loose to graze. As he was a long time his companions were alarmed, and one of them wanted to go off alone to search for him. But then an old and experienced member of the party intervened. He said there were *Almas* living in the saxaul wildernesses in that part of the area, and that it was impossible for one man alone to go and look for their absent companion.

So three of them set out to find the missing man. As they were combing the saxaul thickets they came upon a cave in a sand-stone escarpment. At its entrance they saw signs that a man wearing boots had struggled with a bare-footed creature. Terri-fied, they did not dare enter the cave, and collecting their camels which they had left to graze nearby, they went back to the camp to get guns.

However, the veteran caravaneer dissuaded them, saying that once an *Almas* had caught a man, it would be some days before the creature came out of the cave again. Consequently, it would be futile to keep watch over the cave. He said: "The *Almas* does not kill people it catches. We will continue our journey, and we will free our friend on the return journey because then the *Almas* won't be on watch for us."

On the return journey they did pitch camp near the lair. Three of them with rifles went and hid in the bushes near the mouth of the cave. Nothing showed itself all day, but at sundown some-thing on two legs appeared in the opening, its whole body covered with hair. Shots rang out, and killed the creature outright, and the three men, reloading their guns, rushed inside the cave where they reckoned they would find their friend and rescue him before the sound of the shots could bring out any other *Almas*. They found him, but he seemed totally wild, and quite apathetic as regards their sudden appearance.

The saved captive became strangely silent, and unwilling to say what had happened to him while he was living in the cave. On his return to his home he avoided looking at people in the eye, and often turned away and sat facing the wall when he saw that they were watching him. Two months later he died, which showed clearly, according to the narrator, that some sort of anguish had been consuming him.

The narrator who had told Gopil that eerie story, was an old man called Tseden, and he was well over sixty years old then in the mid-nineteen-thirties. The case had occurred on the southern borders of what today is the Province of Övörhangay.

Another old man whose name was Gendun, and lived at Hüremaral Somon, in the Bayanhongor Province, told an unusual but less chilling story. A short time before the liquidation of the monasteries in 1937, he had seen in the temple of the Barun Hüre monastery the skin of an *Almas* nailed to the ceiling. The stretched skin had been removed from the *Almas* by a long cut along the back, so that skin and face were complete. The extended extremities resembled human arms and legs. The swarthy face was wreathed in hair which hung a long way down. The skin was covered with paintings executed by the Lamas, and dotted with mystical incantations and spells. Gendun did not remember having seen a covering of hair on the body.

The old man who seemed a mine of local information said that in the monastery of Lamyn Hegen, there had lived a certain lama famed for learning. He had been a contemporary of Gendun's father. That lama had been known by the title of "Son of *Almas*". The father of that learned lama had once been captured and held prisoner by some *Almas*, and he begot the boy with a female *Almas*. He managed to escape taking the boy with him, and joined a caravan that happened to be passing. The boy was subsequently given to the monastery,

60

where he became famous for his high intelligence and his erudition.

Gendun then told stories of a certain type of Almas who lived in burrows. According to old and experienced caravaneers, they were known as Nühni-Almas, meaning "Burrow-Almas". The caravans travelled to the town of Hsi-chou and crossed the Gobi Desert in the vicinity of the Matsungshan Tract. There Dambidja, an adventurer-pioneer, had built his fortress and he possibly engaged in other exercises apart from fort-building.

Professor Rinchen suggested that probably over the past twenty years, passage of military units, construction of a railway line across the Gobi, and the widespread development of motor traffic and associated factors, have scared away wild creatures.

He exampled the wild tahi (Prjevalsky's horse), and the wild camel, the havtgay. There were animals at risk in the ever-encroaching civilisation of the wildernesses. "I as a Mongol, am most unwilling to call our native animals by names given to them by chance travellers," he said, "And our wild camel, the havtgay, is still, God be praised, not named by any zoologist, and a few still exist in the Gobi, very few. All this has forced the unfortunate Almas to leave their accustomed areas. It is very possible that the Almas who are thus fleeing before Man, are scarcely more numerous than the tahi and the havtgay, and have already crossed into the realm of extinction. For you see, in the Gobi, from tempests and lack of fodder, it happens that thousands of head of flocks and herds die, even including the fleet-footed dzeeren, the antelope, whose famous speed cannot save him.

"It is possible that if an organised search were made with experienced Gobi trackers, whose sharp eyes and alertness seem fantastic and supernatural to the town dweller, it would be possible to discover, if not live Almas, at least traces of their recent existence.

"During the course of the last few decades herdsmen in several places in the Gobi have seen silhouettes of Almas in the pre-dawn darkness, and have seen by day the footprints on the paths they followed. It is possible to expect that bones, crania, and other

61

evidence could be found there, given the extreme dryness of the Gobi. As late as 1951 in Kobdo Province, the Provincial Authorities reported that *Almas* were encountered.

"If, despite the conservatism of many authorities, the scientists' search for the 'Snowman' in the Himalaya is crowned with success, let them remember that there was a time when the Mongolian *Almas* could have been discovered much sooner, and with far less expenditure of time and effort, were it not for the inertia of those to whom with full justification the old Mongolian curse might be applied: 'Ah, would that thou thyself hadst never known and had never heard the words of those who know!'"

A sidelight on the strange official inertia of non-cooperation the world over, is reflected in the following comment, also from Professor Rinchen: "At one time I had to supply my own paper for recording folk-poems and other folkloric texts, as the administrators thought it a waste of paper to give any for such useless purposes as my notes on folklore. And although up to 1937 I still continued to collect any chance information I could find on *Almas*, I no longer had any hope of ever being able to devote myself to the problem—now resurrected—of *Almas* existing in the Gobi region."

Perhaps now, in view of current field work, Professor Rinchen and Professor Kofman will meet on common ground?

CHAPTER EIGHT

Back to Himalayan Scenes

When recording a sequence of adventures in research, it is cogent to sustain continuity and the central interest by returning at obvious points to that first centre of interest and information.

So this returns to a familiar link in the present history to the well known but immense area of the Himalaya, where the Snowman mystery was first presented to Western opinion for its conjecture or rejection.

The people of the kingdom of Bhutan believe to this day in the existence, at least in the near past, of the Snowman, the Himalayan elusive image that has been the subject of reports, alleged sightings, legends, and scoffing denials of its existence. The many experts who were sceptical, and still are, demand physical proof. Other experts sit on the sidelines, or give views that "there is something".

That "something" may perhaps be eventually divulged as scarce and "fringe" near-human distributions exploding all other theories, and perhaps making *homo sapiens* feel rather outraged, or rather small. The current Russian research may substantiate that theory.

If that ever happens, it will be the "establishment" views of West that will be confounded, for all our advance in Science, and not the naïve simplicity and often strange beliefs of the East.

The beliefs in Bhutan's mountain kingdom are simple, fairly down-to-earth, and convey a sense of unworldly yet practical honesty. They are unshaken in the knowledge that in remote and often inaccessible regions of their beautiful, but now progressively emerging country, a few rare specimens of the mystery entity wander. Several yak herders have claimed to have seen it, or to have discovered its track when crossing high snowbound mountain passes.

Their present generation, they say, have seen fewer Snowmen, and the reason for this is that the rare species is on the verge of becoming extinct.

Snowmen are pictured in old Tibetan and Bhutanese religious scrolls, manuscripts, and monastery murals. Certain engravings are in evidence, taken from once active centres, and from Mongolian temples—their distant neighbours. Tapestries are preserved where the same design occurs. This design takes the form of various images and types of the "Hairy Man," differing in some respects from his fellow-animals. These animals are depicted pictorially next to him in their recognisable zoological shapes.

The Bhutanese believe in three distinct types of Snowmen, or Yeti, as do most remote communities in the high Himalaya. Their Yeti tallies closely with other Himalayan beliefs, and with some in the other regions I have already presented.

Snowman Number One is large and fairly docile; the second type suggests a savage carnivore, about five feet tall, long-haired and apelike, and of muscular build. Thirdly, comes a "Little Man", shy and shaggy. But the Snowman image that gained popular recognition as the Yeti, is the savage, so-called "Ape-Man" that leaves footprints above the snowline at altitudes ranging from 15,000 to 25,000 feet, or in soft ploughed land or sand. From speaking to explorers who have seen the footprints, I believe the highest altitude where tracks were found was 22,000 feet.

According to the most recent statement I received from Bhutan, various types of Snowmen have common characteristics. The pungent smell, and the high whistling, or mewing call, tally with some of the features attributed to other similar mystery creatures.

Interest in the Abominable Snowman and the "Hairy" creatures that may be the Snowman, or its close relation, comes ar goes, but it always revives, and it increases whenever an incident occurs that recalls various stories, expeditions, and abortive searches.

64

Why there has been so little confirmation or definite rejection, is because Yeti research is generally included in Himalayan expeditions mounted for other objectives. In such recent attempts, the idea was to track a Yeti, photograph it, and capture it without inflicting any harm. After scientific study—under sedation —it would have been released, allowing it to return to its natural habitat.

A pipe dream so far. None of the expeditions succeeded in bringing back any concrete evidence, in spite of collecting and sifting much fact and fiction; mostly fiction according to the Western world. But that has not shaken the beliefs of the inhabitants of some Himalayan regions. Even in the West there are a few informed people who have thought in line with the mountain dwellers. By some accounts, this might tally as a rare animal, not unlike the mountain gorilla of Africa.

Civilisation infiltrating in some remote nations, may provide valuable progress, but there might be also some doubt as to ultimate benefit of that progress, in view of warring ideologies, dissensions, and lethal actions some so-called civilised peoples inflict on one another.

One of the features civilisation has unwittingly imposed upon some emergent nations is an inculcation of shame at their past traditions and folk-cultures. So that even in the Himalaya, though not in Bhutan itself, there is a tendency to deprecate the imagery in their histories as superstitious myth in an attempt to achieve modernity. Ours are civilised savage years. Many tenets of an enlightened evolution are poor substitutes for simplicity of thought, and for the ideologies of ancient and perhaps more honest pasts.

The Bhutanese culture, based on very old drawings and paintings were reflected on the tenth of October, 1966 in their Posts and Telegraph Works, and their stamps. This national gesture took the form of a commemorative series of Snowman Stamps in five designs and representing different values.

The Snowman is the "national animal" of Bhutan.

The Bhutanese issued other very beautiful stamps, of local flowers, and they were the first to create an exquisitely coloured stamp to celebrate the space age. Nonetheless, it is their Yeti stamps that stand out quite spectacularly as their national emblem. They are designed by Bhutanese artists and are striking in their colourful, triangular-shaped concept (*see opp. p. 56*). Figures of the different Snowmen types appear against backgrounds of green, rose-coloured, buff, orange, blue yellow and purple. The medium-sized man-eating Yeti's likeness was copied from a mural in a monastery in Northern Bhutan. He is a fearsome looking brute, angrily copper or yellow. Some of the depicted Snowmen have china-blue faces, artistic licence probably. They all possess the typically pointed skull of the Yeti, described by various witnesses of theorists from time to time.

Two denominations of these stamps denote the large Snowman reputed to kidnap victims, generally girls. The stamp picture actually shows him in the act of doing just this. I understand that this large Snowman image tallies with descriptions of the mythical snow-lion of Tibet. Another ancient scroll painting on which the artists relied shows an ape-like Yeti. The Bhutanese call that one the true Himalayan Yeti. The drawing gives an oddly human anatomy in full. Some of the others only present head and shoulders. The true Yeti stamp depicts a figure sitting cross-legged against a distant snow peak. Its upper part is distinctly female, but a sort of tail is apparent, artistic licence again. To my knowledge no tail has ever been attributed to the Snowman, except in a discredited story of some years ago. In that yarn, two Scandinavian travellers were supposed to have reported that they were attacked by a long-tailed Yeti on a mountain pass. They were alleged to have gone to a Darjeeling hospital to have their injuries attended to, but no-one at that hospital would ever confirm their visit.

The "Little man" Snowman stamp is rather endearing, representing the head and shoulders of a half grinning, half apprehensive, small creature, with spiky hair and a hairless face except for a few stiff wisps sprouting around the chin. The face is sharply divided into one dark and one light side—a double personality? Another version, "The Old Man of the Snows", is venerable, and the most human-looking Yeti stamp picture. He sits cross-
66

legged, very hirsute, and white-bearded, holding a hand up to a seemingly weary head.

[At the risk of being indicted for flippancy, it must be said that the "Old Man" Yeti stamp from remote Bhutan rather called to mind *Walter Gabriel*, an inimitable character of the Archer Sound Radio saga, so clearly portrayed for the mind's eye by actor Chris Gittens].

But humour (if misplaced) apart, the Snowman theme lingers on in that mountain kingdom. No recent physical evidence of its existence is available, but Doctor K. Ramamurti, Bhutan's Postal Adviser, who has given me valuable data, told me of one interesting encounter with a Yeti a good many years ago.

A close relation of the King of Bhutan, His Majesty Jigme Dorji Wangchuck, is reported to have seen a Yeti once when out in the open country of mountainous forests.

No other details of her sighting are available, but this would count as the only glimpse a human being has had directly of the mystery creature, except for the brief sighting Tombazi had in 1925.

Perhaps continued field work in widely separated places may eventually apportion their correct labels to the Yeti, the *Almas*, *Van Manas*, and the *Bigfoot* of Northern California whose very odd repetitive story will be told in a later chapter.

If rare and hitherto unidentified species could be proved to exist, however fantastic the discovery, however dwindling the breeds, perhaps the *Fauna Preservation Society* could help to save one or two from extinction as they have done with the Arabian Oryx.

Admittedly, the operation would be fraught with problems. Capturing the Snowman or Snowwoman, if they did turn out to be physical fact, might not be so pleasing as the saving of the graceful Oryx, or even as the lassooing and taming of the mountain gorilla in Africa.

The question, like a recurring decimal, keeps returning: Is this zoology, anthropology, or a rare "twilight" factor embarrassing to Science?

CHAPTER NINE

Fringe Reports and Incidents

One story, indicating belief in the Himalaya in the bi-pedal Snowman species, has been given varied versions down the years. No claim is made here for its entire accuracy or for the impression the incident made on the first travellers who must have seen something and told the story. For stories have a way of snowballing into fantasy with the passage of time. But this report travelled from mouth to mouth, and has been quoted more than once in print.

Pilgrims and others who went to shrines in the Himalaya would tell visitors that a race of giant men existed in the mostly unexplored vastnesses of the mountains. They were neither bears nor apes. Some witnesses stated they had seen them far away between inaccessible peaks and valleys, and that they spoke in an unknown tongue. That must have been a stretch of the imagination considering the distant sightings.

Tibetan monasteries would often speak of the unknown "wild men", and said that traces of them were sometimes found nearby. The lamas of those *gömpas*, as the monasteries are known, would set up a beating of gongs and other noises to terrify them away. One report tells how some yetis were once made drunk, and then set upon and killed while they lay in the *gömpa* compound. But that happened very long ago, if it happened at all.

The debatable story of the "giant men" of the mountainous forests of Nepal speaks of the discovery of enormous footprints, by a reconnaissance expedition, and how they heard strange sounds rising from an unseen valley they were approaching; a roaring sound as of many voices in unison.

They came to a gap in the mountains, and looking down they saw, in a natural circle of rocks below, a ring of about twelve or

68

so ape-like giant men. One of them, seeming the leader of the tribe was beating a very rough tom-tom hewn from a tree-trunk, and the others were swaying to the rhythm of the beat.

The ceremony seemed like some sort of magic or invoking ritual, and the unseen witnesses said that their faces were half like gorillas', half like human faces, though their naked bodies in the icy cold were covered with hair or fur. They appeared to be communicating in unintelligible sounds, and one report suggested that there seemed something tragic and not entirely bestial about them.

Were these mystery half-human outcasts that avoided mankind, or was the whole incident magnified in someone's outpourings of imagination? No one has ever been able to find out, but it is one of the classic half-legend stories of the Snowman theme.

Africa has some claim to a few mystery creatures, though here I can only include one or two with Yeti characteristics. The varied image of the East African tribes' once dreaded *Chemosit*, or "Nandi Bear" is now discredited and relegated to folklore legend with the emerging of African nations into what is known as "enlightenment", (even if the witch doctor is as powerful as ever).

But it is curious that the legendary predator-bogey of Africa's remote areas should be saddled with the same characteristics as are attributed to the Snowman thousands of miles away. The mewing sound it makes, its musty smell, the occasional bi-pedal walk, and its taste for eating its victims' brains.

A Nandi tribesman in Britain demonstrated to me, with a waste-paper basket on his head, how some Africans in isolated and wild country crawl out of huts with baskets over their heads to ward off surprise attacks on their brains by lurking predators. The Elgayo tribe, who were reputed as fearless hunters and trackers, wore straw helmets until recent years when out hunting.

The story that follows was told me by Angus McDonald about an experience he had several years ago. A few features in his encounter coincide with the Yeti picture.

69

As an engineer he was once posted to Kenya on land development operations. The terrain was very remote, and a part of it has remained so to this day, but in an increasingly lesser degree as development expands rapidly.

He and his fellow-engineers' camp was dotted around a place called Kipkabus, completely wild except for scattered tribal communities. They were about one hundred miles from any civilisation and there was no permanent habitation for miles around. The employed tribesmen had their quarters on one side of the camp and McDonald and others occupied scattered huts on the other. The altitude was about 9,000 feet and there was scrub and dense afforestation all around the camp.

In McDonald's own words here is what happened:

"The banda [a primitive hut] had my bed alongside the wall under the open window. One night I was awakened by hearing a noise right under the window. I was throwing off blankets, it could be chilly at night, to investigate, when there was a shriek of rage, quite unlike the sound of hyaena, lion, or leopard, and it was different from any animal cry I had ever heard in Kenya. I jumped out of bed at the same moment as a great hairy body leapt in through the window and landed on the bed almost on top of me.

"I managed to break free, and there followed an indescribable nightmare of a chase. The thing was a bi-pedal most of the time, that I could make out, and it smashed up everything in the banda in our game of hide-and-seek. My three dogs had been outside the hut, but had run off howling in terror. I had only two rounds of ammunition, but anyhow I could not get at them.

"In the bright African night I kept heading off my attacker with anything I could grab, and it kept bumping into me, and pursuing me in and out of the hut. My panic-stricken dogs were barking madly and had roused the whole camp, and now there was pandemonium as everybody began banging on tins and yelling in the workman's quarters to scare the mystery raider away. They succeeded after the longest five minutes in

70

my life, and my hut was a shambles."

As McDonald told his colleagues when they met, an odd feature of the whole attack had been that as the creature charged about on two legs it had been uttering a high piercing scream, mouth wide open. The shape of the head in the moonlight seemed round, more like an ape's than a hyaena, and the creature's height must have been about seven feet. It looked greyish brown in the deceptive moonlight, and it had a strong musty odour, and showed a wide open red mouth.

Next morning the party got in some fresh ammunition, and prepared to track down the animal with dogs and workmen, for spoor had now been found in the clearing. The footprints were roundish and bear-like and ending in digits. The creature had walked on its hind legs and then gone down on all fours and made off into the cedar tree groves around the camp. It did not appear to have any tail and the spoor could not be identified with that of any other known animal. Mr McDonald continued:

"I used to hunt buffalo, leopard, and other big game, but when we got ready to set out on our hunting party, the Africans refused to go with us, and the two dogs, with some instinct of something being *out of order*, also refused to budge. They had been terrified the night before, and they could still smell *something* that scared them.

"Among our men were two Elgayo tribesmen, noted for their prowess as huntsmen, but one and all hung back, and would not track the thing down. They kept repeating with taciturn tenacity that the invader must be given a wide berth because it was a *Chemosit*."

The Chemosit image would occur in stories along the Mau Escarpment which lies on the east side of the Rift Valley. Tradition of the dreaded half-animal, half-supernatural entity has existed for centuries, and almost without exception in regions of similar geographical nature in different areas of the world.

In recording sightings or encounters with the unidentified

71

bi-pedal mystery creature, one must differentiate between the impressions received by inhabitants native to a locality, and visitors or investigators in the same area. The inhabitants' reaction is often coloured by fear and superstition, but that long-past experience of Angus McDonald is authoritative because of his trained upbringing and his profession. This gave him the obvious advantage of ability to be entirely objective, even though he never solved the identity of the thing that attacked him.

His workmen's reactions were rooted in deep racial beliefs at the time. But in their way their attitude counted too. There was a certain similarity there with the reactions of the rather primitive Moslems of the Russian scene, who faced with the far more believable *Almas*, still thought them to be supernatural demons.

Currently, I have heard from Mr McDonald and the incident is still very clear in his mind; he said: "*Chemosit* and *Kereite* were the only names I heard the creature called, and the Elgayo and Nandi were the only tribes I met who spoke of it at all, but to them it was real and to be feared."

Another informant of sightings, or news, of peculiar creatures that walked on two legs is Colonel B. G. Lynn-Allen.

He was once stationed for many years in East Africa, and during that time recorded some very strange stories from tribesmen, white hunters, and settlers. He thought many of the stories, though stirring, were only folklore, and that much of the data could be dismissed as fantasy. But, being intensely interested in all wild life, he was always on the look-out for anecdote and conjecture. Like most newcomers, he got value for his money.

Many Europeans laughed openly at rumours of semi-humans or semi-animals. Yet now and then one met a man who believed firmly there was something in wildest Africa still unknown and unrecognised by the scientist.

Colonel Lynn-Allen said: "The most puzzling feature was not that some creatures should have defied the scrutiny of science for so long, but that descriptions tallied so ill."

He agreed with my comment that contradictory evidence also occurred in the Himalaya over the question of the Yeti, and he continued:

"Some people told stories of a tall ape-like thing that walked upright, while others talked of a large forest-dwelling carnivore which was neither lion nor leopard. It took me some years to realise that there must be two distinct types of mystery creature, varying greatly in shape and size, but somewhat bewilderingly with certain physical characteristics in common.

"To take the large ape-like creature, the only recorded reference to that mystery which I have ever seen was in an excellent story, The Ngoloko, written by J. A. C. Elliot some years ago.*

"Elliot's story was made up from statements purporting to have been made by various coast-dwelling Africans inhabiting the area northwards from Mombasa to the south of the river Tana. The most complete description came from one African, Heri Wa Mabruko, who claimed to have seen many years before near Witu a Ngoloko which had been shot with an arrow from the bow of a Mboni, a member of a primitive Tana tribe. Here is an excerpt from Elliot's fascinating yarn as told by Heri Wa Mabruko.

" 'When I came up he was lying outstretched on the ground, and still breathing. It was a male, about eight feet high, and in breadth just about the same as two ordinary men standing together. He was covered with a mass of long thick grey hair. It was especially long over the head and upper portions of the body, a single hair being quite a yard in length. He was built like a man but was no child of Adam. He had but one finger and one thumb on his hand, the latter ending in a single hooked claw two and a half inches long. The foot had a very large prehensile thumb and three toes, one ending as in the hand in a great claw. The face was hairless, displaying a dark skin, nose very prominent with two nostrils. The mouth was small, but larger than a man's, and the teeth were big. His ears were like those of an elephant and were each about the size of my two hands fully extended when holding the wrists together. The cheekbones were prominent, forehead low and retreating like a leopard's. Chin likewise. I did not notice the

* The Ngoloko by J. A. C. Elliot, appeared in Blackwood's Tales of Africa in their Book IX.

73

colour of the eyes which were big. The eyelashes joined on the hair round the face. The smell was awful and about ten times as strong as a he-goat's.' "

Comment to that narrative could be that it was impressive, but must have been much edited for clarity, and that Wa Mabruko's reference, "no child of Adam" was hardly a remark to expect from such a primitive type.

After disposing of Heri Wa Mabruko, Colonel Lynn-Allen told me of another incident that happened to a friend of his. That friend, a well-known white settler, was, on one occasion hunting elephant near Lake Beringo, which is about four hundred miles from the Witu district. "My friend," he said, "was in thick bush watching for his quarry, and was doing this from one of those small rocky hills that are common features of East African bush country. Suddenly, out of the corner of his eye, he saw what he took to be a tall African walking across a clearing in the bush some six hundred yards away. The upper part of the figure gave a very hairy impression. But a goatskin shoulder cape was frequently worn by older men in that district. My friend told me that beyond faint surprise at seeing a man there, for he was in a more or less uninhabited area, he gave the matter only a passing thought.

"Some time later when the elephant had ceased to occupy his attention, he mentioned the tall man to his African tracker. Upon this, the tracker assured him that the thing he had seen was not human. They searched the clearing and found tracks that were certainly not man-made, but were nonetheless the footprints of some kind of bi-ped. The creature that had made them had passed on."

This is probably the only other evidence of the existence of an African counterpart of the Yeti, the creature, whatever it was, that was once called *The Ngoloko.*

"For me," the Colonel said finally, "the most telling point in this incomplete story was that the tracker had without any prompting volunteered the statement that the thing was not human. Had my hunter friend made the suggestion first, it would in my opinion have decreased materially the value of that tribes-man's identification of the mysterious being, for many Africans of those days were only too willing to agree with a European statement, partly to please, and partly to save themselves the trouble of arguing.'*

Some unidentified sightings quoted from time to time have been more terrifying in their appearance than in their actions, notably, the hairy sub-human looking creatures, considered at first to be large apes, that had occasionally scared easily intimidated forest communities in Malaysia. Then, for nearly one hundred years, there have been reports of forest "primates" in the wild Northern Californian timber belts and in the remotest parts of British Columbia.

Such stories have travelled from person to person at times, witnesses even coming forward to give their tales to some of the more colourful pages of the local presses. But for long, they were not convincing enough in their evidence when questioning came to the crucial point of proof.

The situation regarding the Californian legends may now in the late sixties have altered, and alleged developments there will be examined in later pages, though the reports from America's fruitful West Coast in this case, rather remind me of the famous James Thurber cartoon: "All right, you heard a seal bark!"

Meanwhile coming up is a truly fringe incident recorded here merely as a nonsense story. Entertainment is this report's only value.

The scene was laid in a small township in Michigan, U.S.A., called Sisters Lake.† Fruit pickers said they were being terrified by a monster haunting the swamp forests and coming into the strawberry fields to attack them. The workers were groups recruited from the deep South and Mexico. They refused to con-tinue working, and farmers and their families had to do the picking in view of the fruit's perishable nature. The monster was described as enormous, shaggy, and nine feet tall.

* At the time Col. Lynn-Allen quotes, the area was more or less unexplored, a condition now somewhat altered.

† *Sunday Express*, June 14th., and July 6th., 1964.

Locally it was proposed that the mystery raider might be a very large bear strayed two hundred miles south from the Canadian border. There was panic after a party saw and tried to track the animal. Gordon Brown, a young worker from Georgia, was driving in a car with his wife and two friends, when they saw a huge creature in the radius of their headlamps. It did not move at first, and then lumbered off into the woods.

They tried to follow, but "Our courage failed us", he said, "And we ran back to the car as fast as we could. It was about nine feet high, and stood straight up like a tree. It seemed a cross-breed monstrosity between a gorilla and a bear."

Rain overnight washed out the footprints. But the wife of the farmer who owned the land, Mrs Evelyn Utrup, told police: "I know a large creature exists because I hear it making noises in the night. Sometimes it comes close enough for you to hear its heavy movements, and the farm animals bellow in terror."

Sisters Lake is normally a small quiet community of about five hundred inhabitants, but the *monster* story transformed it into a tourist centre.

So many gun-carrying visitors converged on the little town that Sheriff Robert Dool ordered some of them to leave. He was carrying his own gun as he did so, showing he meant to enforce his order. He was alleged to have said:

"This doggone creature has turned this town into a nightmare. One farmer lost fifteen workers on the day the creature was sighted. They just fled in terror, and it's the height of the strawberry season. Some farmers will face ruin unless their crops are brought in. I had to order hunters away because it's getting mighty dangerous; three thousand strangers prowling about at night with guns . . ."

Wild stories increased in spite of the Sheriff's strong hand attitude. Suggestions came that it was a gorilla or even a "Wild man". Some said it cried like a baby and walked upright—quite a Yeti touch there.

No more was heard of the Monster of Sisters Lake and we can dismiss his incursion here as just a comic relief in a non-comic enquiry.

CHAPTER TEN

A Borneo Echo, and California

Some years ago while on Abominable Snowman research I had some correspondence with Lord Medway who was working on anthropology and zoology at the University of Malaya, Kuala Lumpur.

Though the little story his letter unfolded deals with a creature very much on the fringe of the present record, it has some relationship to it because it touches on one of those widely separated but somewhat associated "radiations" of species.

The living thing described was called in Borneo, the *Beruang Rambai*, and my very obliging correspondent had received some data about it from the wilds of Sarawak. In his letter to me eight years ago, Lord Medway said: "You may remember that we exchanged some correspondence on the subject of the Yeti *Beruang Rambai*, about nine months ago. I thought that it might now amuse you to have a copy of a letter that took about as long to reach me, on the same subject, from a longhouse in Sarawak. It is from Betong anak Kasa. I will give you the original first in case you can get hold of a Dyak speaker."

I have yet to find a Dyak speaker who can translate the whole of the original from Betong anak Kasa, but I can give the gist of what that tribesman said in his letter.

Betong wrote to say how pleased he was to get a letter about the *Beruang Rambai* which lived on the Kelingkang Hills. He made the following points: The creature was called the *Beruang Rambai* because the hair on its arms and on its thighs was about three feet long. Lord Medway said at this point, that that did not help much, and that he did not know what *Rambai* meant. With the root, *ram*, it might refer to head hair as opposed to body hair, in which case the name might mean The Long-Haired Bear. The men who saw the beast were from, what was then, Dutch Indonesia, and their names were Banau and Penyai, both were now dead. Banau and Penyai saw the creature in 1941 on a height known as "Lost Hill", and they tried to kill it. The animal was considered half-beast, half-ghost. Its hair, said Betong, was black and dry, like *Arenga* palm fibres. Its footprints were gallon-sized. [sic] On all fours it was four feet high. On two feet it stood six feet tall. Betong also wrote: "This animal can go on all fours like a beast. It cannot walk upright like a man." This seemed a contradiction of his former statement indicating bi-pedal height.

However, as Lord Medway wrote to me: "I think it is rather a good letter. You might care to send him a picture postcard of a gorilla!"

And he gave me the Dyak's address which I have kept to this day, together with his letter in the Dyak language.

Perhaps I shall chance Betong having moved and send him that postcard after all.

The next event, or series of events, is more contemporary.

In October, 1967, came news from Vancouver, about a sighting in the wilds of Northern California. Sightings of alleged wild unidentified creatures of very large dimensions, are not new in California and ten years ago, similar reports circulated with descriptions of encounters by timber workers and others. These stories, like the ones in British Columbia, always came from remote and sparsely populated country. The *Sasquatch* of the Canadian wildernesses and the *Bigfoot* of Northern California have grown to more or less folklore imagery down the years.

The 1967 sighting implied something far more concrete.

Roger Patterson and a half-Indian companion called Bob Gimlin, stated they had encountered a Snowman, or rather, Snowwoman, near Bluff Creek, California, one of the same areas where sightings were reported ten years ago. What they saw suggested a giant female. They surmised she weighed 350/450 pounds, and stood about seven feet high. Patterson took a film of the creature moving on a ridge of timber and sand skirting dense forest.

The result of this activity was that the 20 seconds film was shown to scientists and reporters, and controversy ensued.

Patterson and Gimlin had stood ninety feet away from the creature when they took the film, and it looked round once before vanishing into impenetrable bush. They said that even with that distance between them the scent of the "Snowwoman" was intolerable.

Some footprints were produced to amplify the sightings, just as plaster casts of such tracks had been shown before when Bigfoot and Sasquatch stories caught the limelight.

Then Ivan Sanderson joined in to investigate and pronounce an opinion. He is a British author who has conducted many prolonged and intensive investigations in many parts of the world, and lives in New Jersey. He has produced weighty books on natural phenomena, and a volume of his on the Snowman theme came out at the same time as my former non-weighty one, neither of us knowing then of each other's research and study of the subject.

Experts in Hollywood said originally that the film could not be a fake with a man dressed up in monkey skins. It was then shown to Dr William C. Osman Hill, in Atlanta, Georgia, a leading British anthropologist and zoologist, formerly Prosector at the London Zoo, and later associate director of the Yerkes Primate Centre at Emory University. When he was in Britain he gave me valuable advice on my own research work, and wrote a paper on the Abominable Snowman findings, quoting Ralph Izzard's theories and mine.

Dr Hill, together with other eminent scientists in America, did not commit himself on the Californian "Snowwoman" latest report.

At the time of the controversy I saw stills of the film, and in spite of the Hollywood statements that they considered the shots genuine, these pictures puzzled me. There was something wrong about the sequence of exposures, the stride and the close thick-looking texture of the fur.

This was even more evident when some months later I saw the film itself, and heard the non-committal opinions of the scientists

79

who, between the film projections, sat around a table discussing it. They included Dr John R. Napier, Director of Primate Biology Programme, The Smithsonian Institute; Dr A. Joseph Wraight, Chief Geographer, U.S. Coast and Geodetic Survey, who is also a Human Ecologist, and Ivan Sanderson himself. Patterson also appeared, together with lay witnesses of separate encounters with similar phenomena. Dr Osman Hill was absent. He had said on a previous occasion before the film came to Britain in a Television documentary: "All I can say is that if this was a masquerade, it was extremely well done and effective." He expressed the feeling that the evidence suggested there should be a mounting of an expedition to Bluff Creek to search for more evidence.

Sanderson's first reaction was to state he thought the film was genuine. He said: "It is a female, judging by the clearly hanging breasts. About seven feet tall, and she walks upright like a human, with straight legs." He enumerated other traits: Shiny jet-black hair, arms swinging when walking, and head hair growing down to base of cheekbones and over forehead to join eyebrows. It must be admitted that that feature of the joining eyebrows was reminiscent of the Ngoloko story.

The face shown on the film is flat and gorilla-like, nose wide and pug-shaped, and eyes small and sunken. The head rises to a crest, and again a comparison occurs: the description of a Yeti by Eric Shipton's Sherpa, Sen Tensing, some years ago. Tensing had described it as having a pointed skull.

In the film, analysis of the creature's movements were shown several times, and in slow motion too.

The scientists watching and debating around their table in that television documentary were puzzled and non-committal. I felt the same. It was not possible to comment definitely one way or the other at that stage in the exercise.

All along I have wondered if the extraordinary incident might be a recent example of hoaxes that might have been played periodically for many years upon adventurous travellers and research workers by local humorists. Could not some inhabitants in that wild and sparsely frequented territory keep the legend of Bigfoot alive from time to time by staging a manifestation

80

which would be subsequently reported in all sincerity by genuine researchers as a new sighting?

Since seeing the film some months ago, an indirect report reached me. When challenged publicly as to whether he had ever seen such a creature as the new feminine Bigfoot, Roger Patterson was alleged to have been indefinite and non-committal.

Fact or fiction?

For years Patterson had been on the look-out for unusual creatures and happenings in wild country. He was more or less an unofficial showman. Had people who made a cult of Bigfoot taken him and Bob Gimlin for a ride?

CHAPTER ELEVEN

A Chinese Link, and The Legends

The long-debated Snowman theme sometimes reveals fresh pockets of connected information. Such information is not always chronological, so regression into past incidents and records cannot be presented in the order in which they happened or were noted. But they can be assessed in their connection with other happenings, and the network of related factors presents a whole picture in which time and geographical guidance fall into place naturally.

A new (to me) collection of connecting links and linguistic and geographical angles came to my knowledge, producing facts about what may once have been a Chinese distribution area. For the new horizon in Snowman research I am indebted to Gordon W. Creighton, M.A., F.R.A.I., F.R.G.S. who is one of the Permanent Committee on Geographical Names at the Royal Geographical Society. He has fluent knowledge of both Chinese and Russian, has studied Tibetan, Mongolian, and Sanskrit, and reads nearly all the scripts in use in Central Asia and the Far East.

When I was working on my former book I obtained some of the Porshnev and Mongolian references although I had nothing so detailed as the Russian data I have been able to use in this book. Gordon Creighton was able to re-assess a great deal for me, discussing his own knowledge of the terrain concerned. This included study of the Russian map of distribution, ranging from areas already quoted in earlier chapters, to the Chinese border.

Interpreted by Mr Creighton, the Russian map-deductions cover, (1) the restricted "base-zone" to which in this century the Yeti is allegedly confined. (2) A much larger zone in which either individuals or groups have been known to appear only sporadically during present times and the recent past. (3) A still larger area, ranging from the Caucasus to Lake Baikal, and as far towards the south-east as the coast of Fukien Province in China. All this shows evidence of Snowman presence in legend and folklore. It reminds too of all the data of Nicolai M. Prjevalsky who, in the last century, explored from Tibet to Mongolia in connection with reports of the Hün-Göröös—another name for the alleged "Man-beast" and reports of the Almas, also described as the half-animal "Hairy People".

Mr Creighton has made independent deductions. Some of them concern a semi-desert terrain in part of Central Asia where Chinese Turkestan (Sinkiang), Mongolia, and China meet. It lies precisely in what is technically known as Zone Two (at 41° 48N 95° 09 E).

There is a ravine there that runs through an area of massive rocks. This ravine, which contains a drinking well, is called in Chinese Hsing-Hsing Hsia. Hsing-Hsing means "stars" and Hsia means "ravine".

"Ravine of Stars" seemed a meaningless and unlikely name for such a place in Central Asia, said Creighton, and it was his research into that misleading Chinese title which led to his discovery of Snowman association with the spot. On finding the name for the first time on the map, he at once remembered another Chinese word, also Hsing-Hsing, which means, not stars, but a species of giant apes.

Only a linguist of great experience in alphabetical orientalism could have unravelled the true meaning of those cryptic characters and discovered this curious deceit which is apparent on all Chinese modern maps.

The misleading name on these maps is clearly a piece of up-to-date rationalisation, which is encountered everywhere in this age. The modern Chinese, like many other races, say that they don't believe in 'superstition' or 'old wives' tales. Everybody knows, of course, that there are no Hsing-Hsing apes in China. They don't exist, never did exist, they are pure mythology, inherited with so much other rubbish from the unenlightened and unscientific past. That is their attitude.

83

So, today, the emancipated Chinese know better, and have decided that the name of that forbidding ravine can only be "Ravine of Stars".

Such disclosures are in character with the efforts of killing all myth, tradition, and folklore by certain newly-emerging nations in many parts of the world. The instigators are unaware that they are destroying a richness and interest that should be preserved from the very weave of their history and geography.

During checking on the reputation of that Ravine of the Apes, Mr Creighton consulted a famous dictionary compiled in the eighteenth century for the great Manchu Emperor, K'ang Hsi. This book is the equivalent to our Oxford Dictionary, and is unrivalled in interpretation of the Chinese language, even if some of the interpretations might be a little startling to Western eyes. It has an entry for the Hsing-Hsing "ape", recognising its existence, but the description of the creature is extravagant enough to remind one of the excusably eccentric entries of Pliny the Elder in his writing on natural history. According to the Chinese Emperor's dictionary the Snowman had a face of a dog and the build of a man, and its cry was like "the wailing of a small child". Again, a characteristic attributed to the Yeti.

Science today does not admit the presence of the ape species anywhere in China.

But still Creighton felt there was reason to believe that the mythical Hsing-Hsing Ape had in the past not been a myth, and that in China, as in Tibet, there had been traces of ape-like man, or man-like ape.

Creighton said:

"Not long ago I found out what I consider to be a good confirmation for my own purely intuitive conclusions. I was reading a book by a Chinese diplomat, Chang Hsin-Hai, who had been a former ambassador to the U.S.A. and to several European countries. That book is The Fabulous Concubine,* the true story of a Chinese woman who rose to be mistress of a Chinese Ambassador to Russia and Germany. She played an

* Jonathan Cape 1957.

important role amid the intrigues and excitements of the Boxer rebellion in 1900.

"Strangely enough, the book contains a reference to the *Hsing-Hsing* Ravine. It is written in English and the passage is interesting enough to quote: 'We came to the Ravine of the *Gorillas*, believed to be a dried-up river bed, where, so the story goes, man-eating gorillas came down from the surrounding mountains to drink.'

"Ambassador Chang Hsin-Hai, like myself, was interpreting this place-name as the *Hsing-Hsing*, meaning a gigantic ape of some sort, and *not* as the Hsing-Hsing, meaning, 'stars'. It is clear by the words the author put into the mouth of one of his characters that there is a tradition of the Yeti associated with the ravine. That Chinese diplomat rendered 'Hsing-Hsing' as 'Gorilla', and in fact if a modern Chinese dictionary is consulted it will be found that the term 'Gorilla' is '*Ta Hsing-Hsing*, meaning 'Big *Hsing-Hsing*'. This shows that when casting around for a word to render 'Gorilla' (an ape of huge size found only in Africa) the Chinese found no other term for it but this one of '*Hsing-Hsing*' which was used in past times to describe a gigantic, allegedly mythical man-ape encountered in the region of this ravine, and also in various other places, as the dictionary compiled for K'ang-Hsi showed. All this knits together. I submit that the '*Hsing-Hsing* can only be the Yeti.'"

What is particularly interesting about this is that one of Gordon Creighton's reasons for believing in the "Ape" connotation of the name of this ravine was the fact of its very close proximity to the border between China and the far south-western extremity of Mongolia. As already shown in Chapter Six, the present-day Mongolian investigators of the *Almas* all say that the creature has now withdrawn towards these more inaccessible regions of western and south-western Mongolia, and that other areas of Mongolia are today free of them.

The *Hsing-Hsing* Ravine being close to this particularly inaccessible and uninhabited region of Mongolia, it is likely that in previous centuries, the *Almas* were a dangerous hazard to travellers through the Ravine, using the south-western corner of Mongolia as their base and raiding over into the Ravine which lies in Chinese territory.

A Sino-Swedish Expedition (1927/1935) was led by Sven Hedin. In the Sven Hedin Foundation 1968 reports on Central (Asian Atlas *Memoirs on Maps**) there is an interesting reference in the Index of Geographical names: Under the place-name "Hsing-Hsing-Hsia," some of the features described are drinking wells, a temple, and a military post, and there is data of a railway station existing there situated on the railway line recently laid from Lanchow (China) across Sinkiang to Kazakhstan in the extreme south of Russia. This work had been helped on by the Russians at a time of rather closer co-operation between the two countries. But the point here in quoting *Hsing-Hsing-Hsia* again is because this Index, which can be termed irreproachably correct, gives the definition of the place as "Defile of the Apes" contrary to the modern Chinese rationalised definition of "Ravine of Stars".

This certainly appears to make Gordon Creighton's interpretation fact and not surmise.

There are more scattered Chinese records of sporadic "wild man" or Yeti glimpses. One of these stories was quoted by the *Peking Daily*† of 29 January, 1958. A Chinese film director, Pai Hsin, of the Chinese People's Army film studies, saw Snowmen in the Pamirs, in 1954, at an altitude of 6,000 metres.

Soon after sunrise one morning on return from film location in the Himalaya he and his three colleagues suddenly distinguished two short "men", backs hunched, following one behind the other up a slope a fairly short distance away. Pai Hsin and his companions shouted, and fired shots in the air, but the two

---

* 1968 edition of Reports from the Scientific Expedition to the Western provinces of China under leadership of Dr Sven Hedin. Vol. II. "Index Geographical Names" by D. M. Farquhar, G. Jarring and E. Norin.

† Picked up by the Communist Chinese News Agency (Hsinhua News Agency, in London, 30/1/58).

"men" paid no heed and went on climbing. They seemed to progress with ease and finally disappeared among the rocks.

On another occasion Pai Hsin and a photographer discovered footprints of a two-legged creature in thick snow. They were similar to human footprints but bigger. They followed the marks for 1½ kilometres, and found some drops of blood on the path. A day's pursuit finally led them to a massive ice-covered rock, but they had to return because it was now too dark to go farther.

On yet another occasion the frontier guards with whom Pai Hsin was staying, on the Sinkiang/Russian border in the Pamirs near Mount Muztagh Ata, threw out some meat. A cow had died of a disease, and they considered the meat tainted. They left it lying there about some 40 metres from their hut and in the small hours in bright moonlight, the guards saw a "wild man" pick up the meat and run away with it. They described the creature as wrapped in white fur, but that could have been an illusion due to the moonlight.

Pai Hsi added to his reports that there were many local legends about the "Wild man" in the Pamirs. He concluded: "Whatever the name of this strange creature, I believe, from my own experience that it really does exist in the Pamirs."

The Chinese film director's experiences have a connection with a much earlier experience in the thirties. A German author, Georg Vasel, wrote a book called *My Russian Jailers in China*,* which contained photographs of the *Hsing-Hsing* Ravine. There could be associations there too with *The Mani Kabum*, the legendary chronicle submitting that the Tibetan people are the descendants of a union between the Monkey King, emanation of the Tibetan deity, Chenrezig, and a female creature "that dwelt among the rocks". The link would be remote, since the legend was located south of Lhasa, a long way from the Chinese Hsing-Hsing-Hsia. Still racial sagas travel great distances, and what could be called "the folk-rhythm" is often related. For instance, in some parts of Tibet alleged demons in ancient times were given the general name of "Srin-Po". All sorts of evils and unexplainable mysteries

* Publishers: Hurst & Blackett, London 1937.

could conveniently be laid at their doors, much as the South African mythical "Tokalosha" can be blamed for anything from hauntings to hate, and be held responsible for the breaking of a china service or of a marriage.

The Srin-Po images equate at times with the Rakshasa of Sanskrit literature. Those Srin-Po were similar malignant nocturnal or daylight entities that disturbed and injured pious folk. They could be distorted traditions of the Yeti, or Mi-Gö, I think there is a link between all these images. The *Raksha* (singular term) is another of the Yeti images, as mentioned already in connection with the epic, the *Ramayana*, Sri Valmiki's poem where the exiled Prince Rama and Sita, his bride, figure in a drama of good battling against evil, and where all that is bad and destructive is personified in Ravan, King of Ceylon, (known also as Lanka), and King of the dreaded *Rakshasa* demons.

Among remote and uninformed communities there has always been the tendency to attach an aura of the supernatural to any living entity that frightens them by not quite conforming to preconceived ideas, and by not providing an explainable solution for simple minds. One case in point being the disturbed Moslem mentioned in an earlier chapter who, in spite of evidence that the *Almas* he sometimes encountered were solid if unusual, still felt that they were *Shaitan*, the devil himself.

The Tibetan legend claims that the mythical couple, the Monkey King and the female rock dweller, were ancestors, and draws attention to a curious physical trait. Gordon Creighton commented on how many of the Tibetan Lamas he had met on his travels had incredibly high-domed and pointed heads. The Yeti of the Himalaya has been described consistently as having a pointed domed skull. In support of this he showed me a photograph taken when Sir Charles Bell, the great expert on Tibet, was in Peking in about 1935. Creighton was present at the function the photograph commemorates and it shows Sir Charles in the company of a number of distinguished lamas of the entourage of the Tashi Lama (also known as the Panchen Lama). The domed, pointed skull, is quite noticeable in the lamas in that group.

Possibly this is only coincidence but the inordinately high

almost pointed skulls of these lamas reminds me of the story, already told earlier on, about the scholarly lama who was known as "The son of the female *Almas*".

CHAPTER TWELVE

Part-Legends and Later Facts

"A long time ago the world begun." Shakespeare put those words in the mouth of Festes, the Clown, in *Twelfth Night*.

Down the ages jesters have clowned and joked, and often spoken in satire and in unconscious knowing of what became part of a truth long after.

Pliny the Elder in his natural history conjectures produced some fantastic zoological and anthropological assumptions. For all their atmosphere of legend mixed with authoritative tone, some of Pliny's inadmissable assertions occasionally connect with beliefs that persist to this day and age relating to certain fauna and debatable creatures in remote and undeveloped terrains, including India's Yeti territory. Some of his writings describe beliefs and stories that still circulate among a few primitive communities. He wrote how in some mountains of the sub-continent dwelt certain tribes possessing eight toes, and feet that turned backwards. The trait of backward-turning feet tallies with the often repeated tale in the past that the Himalayan Yeti's feet turned backwards the better to grip difficult surfaces when climbing. There is mention of this belief among the older Russian records too; the link with the story of the bow-legs and inward-turning feet of the *Almas*.

Cave dwellers and satyrs appear in Pliny's "unnatural history" essays. He spoke of people in India he called the *Catercludi* who were hairy and forest-dwelling and sometimes walked on all fours. Probably Pliny's cave and forest inhabitants were actually langur monkeys. At one point in this excerpt from his encyclopaedia, he quoted a contemporary traveller-writer named Duria, who informed him of certain tribes he had met in his wanderings who mated with wild animals, producing offspring, half-human, half-beast. (Volume 11, Book VII).

After dismissing far-fetched claims, it can yet be put forward that some facets in history's legendary writings can sometimes become the factual history of tomorrow.

In comparison with records of great antiquity the more recent themes of Yeti and *Almas* suggest that in spite of statements that call for rejection, others are not entirely inadmissable when seen in the light of present-day field work and its protagonists' reassessment of past reports.

A popular atlas exists with text and illustration of earth and its geological ages. There is something about the vast eternity it conjures up in the mind that shatters one's self-assurance. The confrontation reduces the reader's estimation of himself to the smallness of the amoeba—the beginning, the first life-stirring. The primal Pre-Cambrian and Cambrian geological divisions are marked "No Life". As one looks up and up that evolving scale of millions of years covering myriad movements and earth alterations, it gives a sense of awful silence of the first ages of this planet. Gradually comes consciousness of the receding or advancing waters, the clearing of the enveloping gases, sound beginning in land convulsions, storms, and then—the amoeba. The separate live unit, unattached to the captive sea-plants.

To span thousands of centuries and reach Neanderthal Man there might be reason to reconsider the established belief that his species died out in the light of sporadic Snowman mysteries. And records of the factual, but periodically suppressed reports about *Almas* and other relevant cases, might be the answer to "missing link" theories.

When major discoveries occur in the history of mankind there is bound to be prejudice and cautious climates of opinion that vote for the safety of the *status quo*, until absolute scientific proof arises. Advance is slow because of conditions of thought. It can take many years before established science accepts a new theory.

Pithecanthropus, the *ape-man*, was the hypothetical link between ape and man.

A skull discovered in a South African mine in 1924 was examined by Doctor Raymond Dart, anatomist at the University of Witwatersrand, Johannesburg, He worked painstakingly for many weeks on its study, and the resulting assessment was exciting. Dr Dart found that some features of the skull were ape-like, but others were more human than those of any living ape or ape fossil known. He concluded that he had found a major link between ape and man, and called it *Australopithecus*, the Southern Ape.

World-wide reactions to his discovery and conclusions raised controversy. In certain circles comparison was made with the newly-discovered "Piltdown Skull". Some of the doubts as to Dr Dart's theories were voiced because the features of Australopithecus differed widely from the Piltdown discovery.

As is now widely known, the Piltdown Skull was exposed as a fake in the early nineteen-fifties. It had originally been presented to anthropology by an amateur investigator called Dawson at Piltdown in Sussex. After enjoying its undeserved reputation for many years, it was revealed positively by Professor Weiner of Oxford as a fake.

This illustrates how easily the proven fact of one decade, or even one century, can become the discarded fable of later times—probably a good explanation of why possible truths found in so-called records of the ancients are treated entirely as fables by many of the moderns.

Among pronouncements on evolution, Alfred Russell Wallace, naturalist contemporary of Charles Darwin, said: "Every species has come into existence coincident both in space and time with a pre-existing closely allied species. The natural series of affinities will also represent the order in which the several species came into existence, each one having had for its immediate antitype a closely allied species existing at the time of its origin. It is evidently possible that two or three distinct species may have had a common antitype, and that each of these may again have become the antitypes from which other closely allied species were created."

Characteristics of development in species are generally that the same pattern of growing occurs in ancestors and contemporary descendants. It can happen though that an early stage of development reverts to the pattern shown by ancestors whose very early characteristics were different from those shown in their descendants. The species has altered down the centuries, through environmental circumstances and the process of adaptation. And then a throw-back occurs, and the early stages of growth in a species resemble those of far-back ancestors.

The reason for the regression is obscure but the fact is that it happens, and it may well account for the pockets of possibly subhuman life now being investigated.

Thomas Henry Huxley wrote in 1863: "*On Man's Place in Nature*" He stated: "Whatever system of organs be studied . . . the structural differences which separate Man from Gorilla and Chimpanzee are not so great as those which separate the Gorilla from the lower apes, that is, the monkeys."

Just as the original horse was a small roaming quadruped of the great wildernesses, no bigger than a dog or fox, so some of the primates were traced as having derived from small tree animals, insect-eating and timid. The Lemurs and Tarsiers of climbing habits, have delicate, human-like little hands, entirely different from hoof or claw.

Three years before Charles Darwin's *Origin of Species* was published in 1859, skeletal remains were found in Germany and pronounced as Neanderthal. There was opposition as to their nature. There may have been reason, for though it was alleged to be the first Neanderthal discovery in Europe, it was stated by later opinion to have belonged to a much earlier stage in human evolution.

Neanderthal finds occurred in France in 1908 at Le Moustier and at La Chapelle-aux-Saints. There were more discoveries in 1910 at La Ferassie but the La Chapelle find was thought at the time to be the most complete Neanderthal discovered.

Some scientists of the more or less contemporary scene believe that more than 200,000 years ago there lived on earth beings not yet human, but far more like contemporary man than the great apes now distributed in relevant regions of tropical forests and mountains. Their brains were bigger than those that apes have.

93

They used shaped stones, for hunting, and accidentally discovered fire from sparks being set off by friction of their stone chippings. Yet, the *Almas* of much later date were alleged by Prjevalsky not to have known how to produce fire.

Descendants of the beings stated to be not quite human were races that died 20,000 years ago. That is one of the statements relating to this theory. Did they die entirely?

Again and again one must re-examine the Himalayan Snowman, and the *Almas* of Mongolia and Caucasus research. Do the proofs of their existence represent lost pockets of a species more primitive even than the Neanderthal to which they are tentatively compared? The comparison is probably wide of the mark, for Neanderthal Man had more in common with contemporary man than was at first considered.

A theory is advanced by Dr C. Loring Brace, Assistant Professor of Anthropology at the University of California. In February, 1964, he wrote in the *Journal of Current Anthropology* that he considered it a fallacy to suppose that present *Homo Sapiens* wiped out the Neanderthal Man from Europe. He stated that what most people recognise as the earliest known hominids were not, in fact, the earliest.

This could account for the Neanderthal humanity factors being in some cases not so far removed from our own.

But variations of opinion have occurred at different stages of discussion over the position of the Neanderthal, and repeatedly the declaration has come that the Neanderthal hominid fossils found represent a type of life that died without issue.

Science is always probing, and there have been disagreements even among the most qualified experts.

One idea does stand out. Man, or near-man, did not occur in one place only. It seems rash to think that the first signs of the creature that walks on two legs appeared only in a few recognised places. Areas of origin are varied, often widely separated, and yet often show the same features.

In 1931/32 near Mount Carmel in what was Palestine there was a find indicating the once existence there of a population whose morphological characteristics lay between those of

94

Neanderthal and modern man.

G. H. R. von Koenigswald, Dutch scientist and traveller, said in 1963: "While I'm not able to prove the assumption that Neanderthal Man still has descendants in modern mankind, others are not able to prove the opposite...." Professor von Koenigswald is of the Department of Palaeontology, Rijksuniversiteit, Utrecht.

CHAPTER THIRTEEN

Back to the East—Fact and Some Fiction

Professor G. H. R. Von Koenigswald's work in the East, and his finds in Hong Kong and Java much extended fossil knowledge.

Through him and his fellow-scientists, fossil hominids from the Lower Pleistocene of Java yielded unfinished links in the often interrupted chain of creation's discoveries and he himself contributed in a major way to research in that part of the world.

Three different types were identified. Two jaw fragments and teeth evoked great interest, and a find in 1941 was of almost gorilla size, but the structure showing the beginning of a non-animal type of spine suggesting human characteristics.

Next, an excavated skull of a creature in infancy was contradictory to earlier discoveries, by showing ape-like dental features.

The Java investigations taking place between 1931 and 1941 established finds of importance, separating the anthropoid and the human nature of remains discovered. A skull of 1939 proved to be human.

The finds came from Pleistocene age regions of deposits in Sangiram, near a place called Solo. Layers of black clay had, down the ages, developed into deposits in a freshwater lake, known geographically as the Djetis Layers.

One of the factors that caused growing research in the Java Man period, is that both anthropoid and human attributes provided evidence of both distributions. Large teeth of hominid character had been found in that terrain since 1936. In 1941 a large mandible was found and proved that here had once existed a giant hominid, the jaw not much less in size than a gorilla's. These gigantic proportions showed so many primitive characteristics that according to von Koenigswald they could not be regarded as only a side branch of mankind, but had to be placed in a line leading to modern man.

In January, 1968, Professor von Koenigswald in an address he gave at Amsterdam, spoke about two human mandibles found in that same Sangiram region of Java in more recent years and brought to Holland for inspection. One was found in 1953, and one in 1961. He made comparisons between finds in the Olduvai Gorge in East Africa (the "Nutcracker Skull" discovered in 1959 by Dr L. S. B. Leakey and his wife) and those at Sangiram, in Central Java. He drew attention to those sites being the only two areas where, within a single geological section, successions of human types were found. Both places showed peculiarities, such as changes in fauna, and a great variety of early hominids more plentiful than anthropoids.

In Sangiram only a few orang-utan teeth were found, while those of gorilla and chimpanzee did not occur in Olduvai.

It is of interest sometimes to refer back to relevant incidents. Koenigswald's research had earlier included random observations, often productive of the small clue, the indication that leads to more important factors. In 1938 he had discovered three giant molar teeth in a Hong Kong chemist's shop. They lay among a miscellany of popular souvenirs often found on such counters in various parts of the world, and they were sold to him as curiosities.

Such a purchase led to long and painstaking field work *in situ*. The Hong Kong teeth were three times as big as a gorilla's, and six times as big as the teeth of modern man. Their formation suggested they had belonged to a gigantic being in a state of evolution half-way between ape and man and they were calculated to be between 450,000 and 550,000 years old.

In such hunting for clues to mankind's mislaid, or conveniently forgotten links, the hunter eventually has to return to key points brought to light previously.

Of such is the journey now from the Java Man terrain back to China from where Snowman, "wild men" and giant gorilla reports have been quoted earlier in this book.

Chou-K'ou-Tien means the Chou Pass Inn, and it is a limestone cliff thirty miles south of Peking in China. It has deep clefts that long were the haunts of "dragon-bone" collectors for the Chinese pharmacies. So-called "dragon-bones" possessed virtues which from ancient times made these relics very popular. Average customers or sightseers often overlook the rarer shop curiosities which only appeal to more informed or merely more curious customers.

In 1931, in a Peking drug-store another tooth of interest was found, this time by K. A. Heberer. It was recognised as fossil man's. Even earlier, in 1927, Birger Böhlin, Swiss palaeontologist, had found a similar molar *in situ*, and Dr Davidson Black, Anatomy Professor at Peking University, named the finds *Sinanthropus Pekinesis*.

So Peking Man, following Java Man, began his journey towards recognition.

From 1927 to 1937 Chou-K'ou-Tien, the site of origin, was worked continuously. Dr Davidson Black being responsible for the research together with Père Pierre Teilhard de Chardin, the famous French priest-scientist, and Mr U. C. Pei. [I plead indulgence if any professional status of the latter is not quoted, as I could not find any at the time of my own searching].

Before excavations were terminated they were joined by the German anatomist, Franz Weidenreich, famous for his studies of fossil man in Europe.

More and more Peking Man remains were found.

All the skulls, teeth, and fossil specimens of Chou-K'ou-Tien were preserved by the team, and Davidson Black was widely named as the protagonist. In 1934 Dr Black died, and Weidenreich was persuaded to take charge of future operations. Weidenreich later wrote an important monograph on the remains. A book called, *Mankind in the making–The story of Human Evolution* by William Powells,* refers to the same theme. Von Koenigswald whose own work led substantially to so much research, quite apart from his own direct involvements, also wrote a book relevant to the subject called *Meeting Pre-Historic Man*†.

* Published by Secker and Warburg, 1960.
† Published by Thames & Hudson, 1956.

World War II and the Japanese occupation of China brought disaster to the carefully assembled collection from Chou-K'ou-Tien. All the *Sinanthropus Pekinesis* skulls and teeth were lost, either in some unspecified accident, or while attempts were made to transfer them from Peking to comparative safety aboard S.S. *President Harrison*. No-one knows what happened to them. Later, the Americans, blamed the Japanese for their disappearance, and afterwards the Communist Government of China blamed the Americans.

What remains as a record consists of a series of casts that had been made in the basement of University Museum, Philadelphia, a solitary tooth in Sweden, and a new mandible in China.

Peking Man might have gone aboard some lesser rescue ship at the time when war first started, or he might have vanished in the sea. His remains were one of the first casualities of the 1939/1945 war in the Pacific, half-a-million years after he had died for the first time.

Similar remains may perhaps be excavated at some time or other in those water-eroded cliffs and hill fissures of Chou-K'ou-Tien, or even in the site's most important hollow known as Cave One which Peking Man himself used, and where the best proofs of his existence were found. Or a skin diver, foraging on a sea-bed for other treasure, might pick up again skull or fragments of *Sinanthropus Pekinesis* as far away from his cavernous habitat as that home of his was from the Chinese Ravine of the Apes, or the haunts of Yeti, *Almas*, *Van Manas*, and mountain "Hairy Man" with whom he seemed to have some affinity.

Joseph Dalton Hooker, William Woodville Rockhill, L. A. Waddell, and a forgotten young man, Lieutenant Francis White, were all travellers whose diaries contain items of information on Himalayan experiences and observations.

The value of the naïve and often debatable accounts of early non-expert travellers or tourists, is that they had no axe to grind. They wrote of incidents or encounters without any inhibitions or discrimination.

Some of the more knowledgeable travellers like L. A. Waddell, were painstaking in their observations. Waddell was the one who

99

included the story of the *Mani Kabum*, the legendary Tibetan saga, among his records.

But in more questionable jottings of those days, that somehow found their way into print and survived, comments are found in between the verbiage, that act as clues in a more serious line of enquiry. Even the folklore, which a few emerging nations are preserving provides sign-posts to information of a morphological nature.

I have a theory, which others also hold, which is that some of the myths and fairy-tales of primitive regions have prevented many quarters of established thought from taking seriously any reports of debatable creatures, such as mystery animals or sub-humans. Yet I would not have the fairy-tales erased from the histories of mankind and the living world. These tales have a philosophy, and the occasional grain of truth in their beginnings, as well as providing a rich and often enchanting tapestry of folk myth.

There is another epic of a Monkey King, by the Chinese writer and poet, Wu Ch'eng-En who lived between A.D. 1505 and 1580, and whose work was transmuted into English by Arthur Waley in a delightful book called *Monkey*. And then there is a little-known tale from Bhutan about the sad relationship between the Buffalo and the Yak.

Though this story's place is located on the fringe of fairy lore, it is quoted here because of its gentle and aimiable quality of philosophy; a contrast to the ferocity in some of the records uncovered so far.

As the Bhutanese folk-tale goes, it is an explanation of why the Yak always lumbers along with lowered head, while the Buffalo always raises his. The Yak and Buffalo were once like brothers, but one day some evil spirit made them disagree. They fell out, parted company and the Buffalo was banished from the higher lands to the plains. Afterwards they longed to meet again, and, so says legend, the Yak with his low-bent head, is always looking down towards the plains, and the Buffalo is always casting his eyes upwards to the hills in the hope that he may see his dear old friend again.

So varied are the fables and myths that in early days of travel and research, the men who became well known for their pursuits in the unknown regions must have been hard put to extricate fact from legend.

Ronald Kaulback recorded the finding of mystery footprints in a journey through Burma into Tibet. He relates in his book *Salween* how some of his party of porters said the tracks belonged to terrifying mountain Wild Men who were very real indeed and lived near the high snows.

Fable and fact were mixed in the *Indian Geographical Journal* in July/September 1955. It contained explanations of the various names for the Yeti, and also presented a variety of Tibetan descriptions for witches and mountain water-goblins that seemed to the writer, (but not to this one!) to have some affinity with the Snowman.

But in contrast, one finds far older records, and accurate documentation by Joseph Dalton Hooker, M.D., R.N., F.R.S. His *Himalayan Journals* appeared in 1884 and comprised of two heavy volumes. In Chapter 1 of the first volume he describes how a race of wild men called *Harrum-Mo* were said to inhabit the head of a valley near the mountain passes of Sikkim. The "wild men" avoided human habitations, spoke a tongue nobody understood, used bows and arrows, and ate snakes and vermin which the Lepcha guides, a relatively primitive race, would not touch. Dr Hooker's *Harrum-Mo* information has a link with the reports of the *Almas* of Mongolia, and William Woodville Rockhill's 1891 accounts of his travels in Tibet and Mongolia, support Hooker in his reports of the hairy men of the woods and mountains.

Actually it is remarkable that both Hooker's and Rockhill's local informants were so down-to-earth in their descriptions of the "Wild man" situation, for it has long been local custom to lace fact with fiction. One case in point came from Marco Pallis, the traveller and author who wrote on Tibet and its lamas. In one temple he found an exhibit marked "dragon's egg". A traveller had presented it to the *Gömpa*, and it was an ostrich egg.

And so, many people, like Tombazi, have always been inclined to dismiss reports of anything unusual as "delicious fairy-tales".

CHAPTER FOURTEEN

Porshnev Speaks Again

In 1968 Doctor Porshnev wrote in *Prostor No 5* about what he calls "The Cave-Men dispute" (in Russian, *Bor'baza Trogloditov*). He sent me all his observations and they were followed later by more material in 1969.

One of the experts Doctor Porshnev mentioned was an Orientalist, N. V. Valero-Grachev. Of him he said: "He lived a vast part of his life in Buddhist monasteries and only returned to Leningrad in the 1930's. When he presented reports and manuscripts to our learned circles, he was advised to 'hold his tongue'. His reports dealt with the 'Wild men' of Tibet.

This order for silence is entirely in line with the whole question of how this generally ignored and strange section in the living world's history has been treated.

Porshnev revealed that Valero-Grachev's papers are now lost, and so are his statements written down for him not long before his death in 1960. In his travels Valero-Grachev had heard many cases, and learned of the various characteristics of the *Almas*, or *Mi-Gö*. It was no longer possible for him to entertain any doubts whatever as to this factor's biological authenticity.

"Another of our country," Porshnev continued, "Professor Yuri N. Roerich, son of the artist, and a scholar, who had spent half his life in the Himalaya, lodged with the Academy of Sciences his own data, revealed to him at a more favourable time. This included his own personal impressions of a piece of skin he had himself seen.

"The Austrian traveller and ethnographer, R. Nebesky-Voykovits, wrote down in 1950/53 in Tibet a number of depositions of eye-witnesses which corroborated the statements of Roerich. And the Polish journalist, Marian Belitskiy, collected

103

lots of fresh reports in 1956.

Porshnev gave an older story he was told by retired General Mikhail Stepanovich Topil'skiy. In 1925, the general was a Commissar with troops that had been sent in pursuit of a band of White Army forces retreating through the Pamirs. In the high region of the Vanchsk area they heard tales of wild men from the local people, "Beast-men", living somewhere higher up, but known from their cries and from rare encounters. In the Vanchsk and Yazgulemsk Ranges, the troops found bare footprints in the snow, and ending at the foot of a cliff-face too steep to be climbed by man. They found faeces resembling human ones, containing remains of dried berries and during a battle between the Reds and the Whites, a wounded Red soldier, an Uzbek, reported that as they were firing into a cave, in which Whites were thought to be, a wild hairy man came running out, making inarticulate noises, into the machine-gun fire, and was killed.

"At first," said the general, "I thought it was the corpse of an ape. It was covered with fur. But I knew there were no apes in the Pamirs, and, moreover, the body looked far more human than ape-like, indeed, fully human."

They tugged at the fur and satisfied themselves it was not just a skin worn by a man and their medical officer established it was definitely not a man. Then they turned the corpse over and measured it. It was male and 165/170 cms long. It had grey hair here and there, so it seemed fairly old, but the hair was generally greyish-brown. On the breast and upper part of body, the hair was more brown, and more grey on the belly. On the chest, the hair was longer but less thick; on the belly shorter and thicker. Taken as a whole the hair was extremely dense, but there was no undercoat. The area with least hair was the buttocks, from which the medical officer concluded that it sat like a man. The hairiest parts of all were the thighs and the legs. No hair on the knees at all, and knees very calloused. On the shins less hair than on the thighs, and sparser and sparser towards the bottom of the shins. The whole foot and sole was entirely without hair, but covered with coarse brown skin. Shoulders and arms were covered with hair, getting less towards the hands, but the same hair on the back of the hands with none at all on the palms. The skin of the palms was coarse and calloused.

The neck was covered with hair, but there was none on the face which was very dark in colour, with no beard or moustache and only a few hairs in places on the upper lip. On the fore part of the head, above the brow, there was no hair and on the back of head, the hair was thick, dense, and matted like felt.

The dead creature lay with eyes open and teeth bared. The eyes were dark, teeth very big and even but no different from human teeth in shape. The brow sloped, and the brows above the eyes were heavy, with extremely salient cheek-bones, like a Mongolian. The nose was flattened with the bridge deeply inset. The ears were hairless and slightly more sharpened at the tips than human ears, and the lobes were longer. The lower jaw was very massive, and the chest broad and powerful with highly developed muscles. The torso was not much different from man's, and the sexual organs were similar. There was no difference in the length of the arms or fingers and toes, but the hand was somewhat broader than a human hand. The foot also was noticeably wider, and it was shorter than a human's foot.

As it was impossible for the soldiers to take the body with them they buried it under a heap of stones.

Back to Doctor Porshnev: "The following statement was given to our Commission by A. I. Malyut, a former Commissioner for State Security in the Vanchsk area, where he worked for six years. Hunters after game such as snow leopards and other animals, made frequent reports about the existence of some man-like being at high altitudes, especially on upper reaches of the Yazgulem River, near the Fedchenko Glacier. . . ."

It will be remembered that the Fedchenko Glacier was where A. G. Pronin saw the wild man on the high rock face.

According to the Commissioner there had been reports of a similar nature in the Bartang area and he said: "It is an interesting fact that apart from that area, I had never heard talk of the Snowman anywhere else in the Pamirs."

Not far from the same locality of Yazgulem village, in the Vanchsk region, at the Fedchenko Glacier Observatory, the radio-meteorologist, G. N. Tebenikhin, experienced certain associated events which, in his own words, he "was completely unable to explain". That was long before the Pronin sightings of 1958; the earliest incident occurred in March 1936.

"Some bi-ped broke a rod" near the Observatory, and then got away easily from men on skis who pursued it for several hours across the glacier. It was brown coloured and it repeatedly sat down and let the pursuers get closer, but never nearer than one kilometre. Finally it vanished down a steep snow-covered chasm, sitting on its buttocks and using its feet as brakes.

Even earlier, in 1933, D. I. Shcherbakov, a geologist, crossing a pass from the Vanchsk uplands to the Yazgulem elevations, saw to his surprise naked footprints resembling a man's. Yet, they were distinguishable from either man's or bear's tracks, by the imprint of the big toe which was bent outwards. This characteristic has often been noticed and related to alleged Snowman footprints.

In 1938, another geologist, A. Shalimov, was on the same pass with a group of Tadjik porters when they pointed out to him the prints of a "wild man" who had passed there quite recently, and had probably been watching the party as they climbed. There again, the big toe's impression was considerably bigger than the rest, and stuck out towards the side of the foot imprint. On another occasion they found bear tracks, and could compare them quite easily as being entirely different from the prints of the 'wild man'.

Once, on hearing of his Pamir sighting, a woman artist, M. M. Bespal'ko, wrote to A. G. Pronin, telling him she had seen the same type of creature when she was sketching in the Pamirs on July 29th, 1943. Similar bi-pedal tracks were reported in the same area in 1958 by Geologist S. I. Proskurko, and in 1960 by a frontier guard named A. Grez, an expert on tracks.

Doctor Porshnev says that on his visit to the Pamirs he made a special study of the Chesh-Tyube area near the frontier in the Eastern Pamirs from which many reports have originated. Southeast of the area he and his colleagues heard of a place where "wild men are still living". This report refers to the Russian

Pamir Expedition of 1958 when they secured a whole series of quite new acounts of the *Adam-Japais*. (A new local name this.) They learned of the newly-discovered habitat from Kirghiz nomads of South-West Sinkiang Province, China.

Porshnev also described friction that occurred once between himself and S. V. Obruchev, about the Snowman. He told Obruchev, a distinguished Academician: "I wouldn't occupy myself with the question if I thought the Snowman was only an ape." And Obruchev replied: "And I wouldn't occupy myself with it if I thought it was a Neanderthal. It is an unknown biped ape."

This was before 1958, the year in which Professor Obruchev changed his mind.

In all humility, and with a still open mind, I must say that a few years ago I too inclined to the anthropoid theory. But not any more.

However this little exchange between these two eminent men is just one example of how divergent such experienced opinions can be.

After touching on Babylonian and Sumerian references to wild men, Porshnev discussed a Russian hunter, N. A. Baykov, who once was a very famous man in Manchuria, where he spent years hunting the great Manchurian tiger, a noble beast, far larger than the Bengal species. "Baykov was a remarkable naturalist and wrote marvellously accurate natural history books." One encounter of Baykov's is well worth recording. In 1914 in Southern Manchuria's forests, an animal dealer called Boboshin took him to a place deep in the forest. There he met an actual 'wild man' who was living in a hut with a Chinese hunter named Fu Ts'ai. Fu was using this strange being as an assistant. Dr Porshnev said, "He had been given the human name of *Lan-Zhen* and he was amazingly successful in catching birds and animals in snares and traps set by Fu Ts'ai. As we read Baykov's account of the 'wild man' we at once recognised, by various signs —the hairiness, the stoping gait, the lack of speech—that we are here dealing with our friend the *Almas*, despite the fact that this particular specimen was clad in the tattered raiments of a hunter.

"The creature was very stunted in height, and seemingly about 40 years old. On his head he had tousled matted hair, which constituted his *hat*! His face, reddish-brown, resembled the face of a beast of prey, and this impression was enhanced by the huge open mouth, in the depths of which sparkled rows of powerful fangs. Seeing us, he squatted down, with his long hairy arms with their hooked fingers touching the ground, and began to mumble animal sounds. His wild, insane-looking eyes shone in the dark like those of a wolf and when reproved by his Chinese master, he replied with a snarl and went over to the wall of the hut, and lay down, curling himself up just like a dog. For a long time I observed this strange being, half man, half beast, and it seemed to me, that he had more of the beast in him than the human.

Baykov took up again in his narrative: "At one time, *Lan-Zhen* (it means 'Wolf-Man') was lying on the floor in the corner when he started to growl in his sleep, just like dogs often do. He raised his shaggy head and yawned opening his broad mouth so that his sharp teeth sparkled. At that moment he was so much like an animal that Boboshin could not contain himself and said: 'Look, heaven forbid that such a monster should be born! Why it's not a whit like a man at all! And if you were to see him out in the forest, you'd be terrified. A wolf, yes, that's it, a wolf. All the ways and habits of a wolf. And it doesn't walk like a man. It's got long, long arms and it often goes down on them and runs on all fours, especially when on the trail of an animal. And it climbs trees as well as any monkey! Yes, and it has the strength of an animal, even though it is squat and puny. Just imagine, even the dogs fear him as they fear a wolf. And it doesn't love dogs either, and snarls at them and bares its teeth. At New Year Fu Ts'ai takes it with him into the town of Ninguta [North-west Manchuria]. All the dogs in the place get excited and bark and howl all night when that monster is there. And they won't let it go along the streets. But if a dog gets caught, it strangles the dog in a trice and bites through its windpipe. Such a nice fellow it is, so obliging. . . ."

During one night Boboshin woke Baykov up and they

stealthily followed Lan-Zhen out of the hut. The moon was shining down on the forest and the snow-capped mountains. The beast-man was squatting under a cedar tree, mouth wide open and head up, giving out the long-drawn howl of a red wolf. With each howl he extended his lower jaw, and as the sound died away, he lowered his head almost to the ground, just like a wolf.

From a nearby hill came the answering howls of wolves. When the wolves fell silent, Lan-Zhen set them off again with his howls. Soon three wolves appeared in the clearing and began cautiously to approach, stopping and sitting down from time to time. Lan-Zhen crept towards them and in every way he gave an astonishingly close imitation of a wolf.

The wolves let him get to five paces or so from them then they retreated into the forest, stopping at times and turning around. Lan-Zhen, moving on all fours, at first slowly followed, and then began running swiftly after them, still on all fours, and vanished into the forest. As Boboshin said: "God only knows what he does of a night there in the forest. Nobody knows, not even Fu Ts'ai, and he wouldn't say even if he did know".

Baykov, taking up his own narrative, said: "Next morning Lan-Zhen appeared from the forest, as wild and incomprehensible as ever. Fu Ts'ai, who was eating his morning meal, gave him the carcase of a squirrel to eat. Lan-Zhen seized it with both hands and began to devour the squirrel starting at the head, the bones cracking between his powerful teeth like straws. Tearing the flesh with hands and front incisors, he squatted there, growling with pleasure".

In this extremely rare case, Doctor Porshnev specified, the process of domestication and training had gone far. "The primitive drank water by scooping it with a dipper from the bucket, although he never learned to sit on a bench. The most interesting feature was that the wild man did not himself eat the game in the forest, but carried it to his master, who took the pelt for himself and gave Lan-Zhen the carcase to eat. Baykov suggested that perhaps the red wolves also would leave him a portion of their own catch".

Porshnev here commented that this unique case might open a

chink into the "for us still closed problem of the position of *Palaeonthropus* in the struggle and strife of the kingdom of life". The species, he contended, was able to raise itself above the bonds of a strictly confined environment. He said: "Zoology teaches us that there are species of *stenobionts*, creatures attached to one ecological zone; and *evrivionts*, i.e., creatures suited to many kinds of living conditions; and lastly, of *ubiquists*, i.e., creatures that live in all zones of nature. The fox, crow, golden eagle, for example."

Palaeonthropus is an ubiquist. He can live anywhere, in any landscape, at any altitude. From certain indications it is deducted that he escapes the effects of cold and lack of winter food by hibernating in caves or in pits that he excavates specially for the purpose, and in which he spends long periods with lowered metabolism and in a state of somnolence. He is protected against the cold not only by his fur but by the layers of bodily fat laid down in the previous autumn. This species is a "devourer of space". Such creatures can run like horses, and swim rivers and fast mountain torrents. In the process of transition to the bi-ped manner of movement, the females, unlike the apes, developed long mammary glands, so, throwing their breasts over their shoulders, they can, while walking along, feed the young hanging on their backs.

Related to the mobility of the species is the fact that it lacks totally the instinct for building a permanent shelter, and instead has only temporary lairs. The zone of distribution of the males is much greater and more continuous than that of the females, yet steady pairings occur during periods of sexual activity. Areas in which young have been seen, however, are extremely rare and localised throughout the world.

"At the present time," said Dr Porshnev, "it is the most rare species of mammals, though it may well be that it once had its own areas of dense population and concentration. The earlier the legends, the more likely the chances of finding stories in them about crowds or herds of such beings. It is reported that near the meeting-points of the boundaries of the Soviet Pamirs with Afghanistan, Kashgaria, India, and Pakistan, they appear in groups of six, or eight, or nine close to inhabited places. The headman of one autonomous district in that region wrote of a whole 'crowd' of ape-like wild men covered with brown fur. And an Afghan teacher gave this account: 'Wild men are to be met in the forested areas of Afghanistan where I was born, either as single individuals, or with young, or in whole bands. They live in the forests. Their food is wild animals. The *Gul'biyavan*, as he is called, is unable to talk, but emits strange noises'.

"Typical of the creature as a whole," said Dr Porshnev "is the scattered distribution over vast areas. But nature has equipped them with means for finding each other. These ways include a powerful and terrifying call which echoes through the mountains after sunset or just before dawn. The species is the same throughout the vast area, but with local variations of height, hair colour, build, etc."

The reader will no doubt remember the name "*Gul'biyavan*" in a previous chapter, and it is interesting to note how that name has travelled quite a distance from the area where it was quoted first in this book. The Doctor's reference to the local variations of type tallies with my previous and current researches, and there is a strong association with all Snowman data.

Doctor Porshnev's extensive studies and field work in the relevant areas comes right up to date with his reports of research undertaken from 1960 onwards. He says: "I took on the job of sorting out the mass of data that we had about these creatures. The result was my *Contemporary Situation as Regards The Problem of Hominoid Relics*. It contained all that was known up to 1960. Next came the even bigger problem of how to get it printed and we ran into every sort of mockery.

"We needed support for the work from outside zoologists and finally solicited the thoughtful and positive analysis of the problem by S. K. Klumov. Another who read the manuscript, N. N. Ladygina-Kots, also dealt with the matter. Then, finally, Professor P. V. Terent'yev, holder of the Chair of Vertebrate Zoology in the University of Leningrad. Naturally, his partial recommendation of the manuscript to the publishers in no way bound him to be my supporter, but he painstakingly checked the scientific text, and he checked it against Linnaeus who has: *Homo Troglodytes*. Henceforth *Homo Troglodytes Linnaeus* they shall be!

"Further warm support came from A. S. Monin, deputy chief of the scientific section of the Central Committee of the Communist Party. and the book was finally published, although only 180 copies were printed with still much opposition from many quarters. Many libraries refused to accept it. But it was OUT. From now onwards it EXISTED.

"But did it? In reality these 400 or so pages of fine print were no more than a 'preliminary report' though a bit longer than the memoir submitted in 1914 to the Academy of Sciences by V. A. Khakhlov. A 'report' to whom? There has not been a single echo in the scientific press, not a review. And that was over five years ago.

"Can it be that it is just one more memorandum possessed of no scientific significance?

"Is it any consolation that the *Systems of Nature* of Linnaeus met with the same fate?

"But we got a new disciple. Dmitri Yurevich Bayanov. It was entirely by chance that he had translated, as part of his duties, my interviews with two correspondents of English papers, and becoming interested in their incredible contents, he went off to the Lenin Library and got out my book, *The Present Situation as Regards the Problem of Hominoid Relics*. Like anybody who reads it from start to finish, he became convinced. And, being young and honest, he could not remain on the sidelines. He began to devote all his spare time and his heart and mind to the subject. And today he is a rising specialist.

"It was Bayanov who drew attention once more to the forgotten writings of Linnaeus about early hominoids although today, the only anthropological service Linnaeus is recognised as having performed is his classification of man along with apes and monkeys in the same order of Primates. Nobody wishes to recall, in all seriousness, what the great Swedish eighteenth-century naturalist understood by the word 'man'. In justification of Linnaeus people now say that the manlike monkeys and apes

112

were at that time quite inadequately studied, and so it was quite easy for muddles and confusions to arise. And indeed in other portions of the *System of Nature* Linnaeus frequently made mistakes, *later to be justified.*

"So how strange it is that under the species 'Man' Linnaeus put not only 'Homo Sapiens' but also two other terms: 'Wild Man' and 'Cave Man' ('Troglodyte Man' in Russian).

"If we eliminate all cases concerning those apes which do resemble man, and cases of children brought up by animals, there still remains, here and there, a tidy accumulation of facts of a different nature. Linnaeus sems to have been in two minds about it, whether to relate them to those of the apes nearest to man, or to 'Homo Sapiens'.

"Here are the main features, which, according to Linnaeus, differentiated these other creatures from man:

1 Their lack of speech.
2 Their hairy bodies.
3 Their faculty of going not only on two feet, but also on all fours."

Yet Linnaeus felt that these characteristics were insufficient for the creature to be classified morphologically as outside the species, "Man".

It appears that D. Y. Bayanov sought out Linnaeus's long forgotten work *On Creatures Resembling Man* which Linnaeus had dictated to one of his pupils. Bayanov found the Russian translation, done by A. Tretiakovksiy and published in St Petersburgh in 1777.

Porshnev concluded: "Bayanov collected not only the cases cited by Linnaeus from the Ancient World and from the Middle Ages, but also a few similar ones Linnaeus had not even mentioned. Inexorably, their ranks loom as they pass in review before the reader. No. Linnaeus was not mistaken."

CHAPTER FIFTEEN

Assessing the Candidates

Towards the end of a record of discovery and re-appraisal of this nature, it is necessary to look back and assess the claims of the various species lined up as candidates. Each central figure in this re-appraisal deserves a second survey.

So one examines these different candidates proffered as possible explanations or actual facts despite the mystery of their survival in remote wildernesses. Their similarities and their differences must be compared again, and the similarities and differences (although there are very few of these) postulated by the persons who followed their sporadic appearances and disappearances in the history of men and animals.

The first candidate is without doubt the Abominable Snowman of the High Himalaya, recorded, doubted, and dismissed, to re-appear and frighten local innocents living in their scattered communities, and to confound the complete pragmatists who said the creature did not exist. Its names of Yeti, *Raksha-Bompo*, *Mi-Gö*, *Dremo*, *Van Manas*, and *Almas* cover *characteristics* that vary at some points, but always tally at certain other salient ones.

The photographs of footprints taken by Eric Shipton (*see opp. p. 24*) caused controversy and "establishment" caution, but they were for many years considered remarkable for reasons other than mere sensation. One of the reasons for not dismissing the tracks as a freak of snow and weather was the human feature of the shape they represented. Many other good prints have been taken photographically, but this one is the sharpest and most factual one. It shows one salient and revealing feature that must be taken into account, perhaps now more than at any other time. That feature is the very large big toe, more human in outline, even in its outward-slanting angle, than shown in photographed

114

footprints of any of the large anthropoids.

This is a contradiction of earlier tentative theories, including mine, that the imprints had been made by an unknown anthropoid, and were not bear tracks, as suggested by several famous experts. But the verdict was also that they were not human tracks.

Meanwhile, investigations which have been fully reported in previous pages, seem to support something very different, the remnant-hominid theory. There is no reason to think that a remnant-hominid, straying accidentally or deliberately from a lair in unexplored mountainous forests and gorges below the snowline, could not reach the altitude of roughly 22,000 feet where Shipton, Michael Ward and Sherpa Tensing found the tracks.

Gradually and against repeated opposition, something has now been brought into the light by field work of the last ten years. It brings the photographic evidence of that much argued huge footprint and its companion track into line.

It also strengthens the theory of my S-Map, produced nine years ago. The whole network of the Snowman's sporadic distribution is found within the world-precincts of that map (*see next page*).

The Snowman distribution situation in the Indian Himalaya is almost the same as the Bhutan position, regarding the myth or fact, whichever it is. There, the Snowman is the country's recognised national image, immortalised in the different types of postage stamps produced for the first time in 1966. The Yeti is described seriously in their guide books side by side with their native fauna, plant, and mountain lore. At times the Yeti is spoken of as the "wild men" by the mountain herdsmen. There is also the report, already quoted, and told to me by Dr K. Ramamurti, of how a Royal relation of Bhutan's King, His Majesty, Jigme Dorji Wangchuck, appears to have been the only person in Bhutan who has actually seen a Yeti. Dr Ramamurti's own words on the subject are: "From what I have heard, no Yeti remains immobile after it is seen by a human. In Bhutan, except for the Royal lady nobody appears to have actually seen a

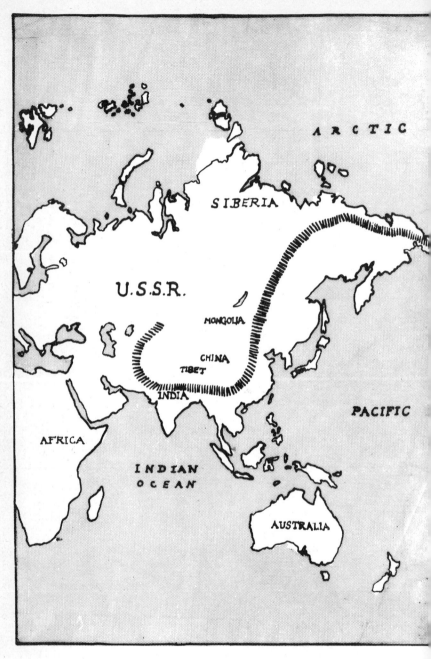

S–Map showing Snowman distribution (see page 115).

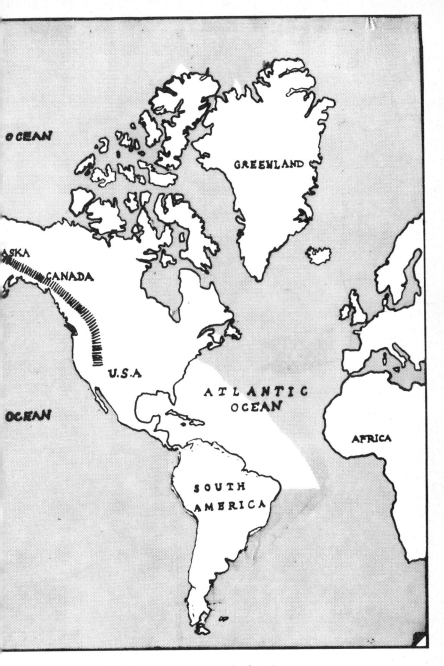

extreme left of "S" lie the Pamirs and the Caucasus

Yeti. She is reported to have described the creature she saw as a '*Mighu*', which means a small wild man. . . ."

By contrast, the Northern Californian Bigfoot episodes must be treated very speculatively. Some of the evidence may provide suggestions of the presence of a very primitive human or animal but proof has been dubious down the years, and not only since the recent mystery "outbreak" and the film. In spite of the sincerity of many of the witnesses, an atmosphere of contrivance surrounds the story. When a report is repeated at intervals, often treated at entertainment level, and heavily built up to stimulate interest, that is the signal for serious research to stand back on the sidelines and wait. The Californian adventure-getters have spoilt what might be a rare root of truth by blowing it up into a forest of levity.

As for its Canadian counterpart, the *Sasquatch*, of once British Columbian legend, it has not yet been mentioned here. There is little to say. The last report I received about that cousin of Bigfoot, was a rambling story that circulated some years ago. It told how a lone worker on the timber line had been kidnapped by a family of strange hairy creatures. He was treated quite kindly, and at last escaped from their rocky fastness. Their inarticulate aim seemed to have been to secure the timber worker as a mate for their young female offspring. But the basis, if basis there is, for that incident must have started long ago, and I cannot vouch for the correctness of the story.

Another very early report must be briefly introduced; this time from South America. Giant footprints were found in the area of the Argentine known as the Salta region, and I knew of these as long ago as when my former Snowman book was published in 1961/63. There has been more recent reference to those tracks, but based on premises outside the scope of this book.

The next re-examination of a candidate deals with the Chapter One Bering Straits "Iceman" freak exhibit of the fair-grounds. Where it lies now cannot be verified at this stage, however, *Bozo*, as Ivan Sanderson and colleagues named the find, was well dissected in words by Sanderson and Bernard Heuvelmans, before its owner spirited it away.

Bozo comes up again here, not only for re-examination, but because a little more research-dissecting has since occurred. It might be of value to look at him again in the light of a new thought as to the Iceman's possible original identity. That is, if those deeply frozen remains were genuinely found in the Bering Straits.

Referring back to Chapter One it may be remembered that there was another version; that the body had been bought in Hong Kong, well known for the occasional sale of curios of an anthropological or zoological nature.

Might the creature have been an unusually hairy Ainu after all, the victim of an attack when hunting or fishing, and (1) been dumped overboard by an assailant, and so drifted to where it was finally discovered, or (2) sold, after being artificially ice-enclosed, to a collector in dubious quarters of Hong Kong so that someone or other would be rid of incriminating evidence?

The Ainu are racially close to the once ancient Neolithic inhabitants of Japan. They are very reduced in numbers and live in Hokkaido; some also used to live in a part of Sakhalin, and the Kurile Islands. This region is north of Japan but under Japanese rule. The Ainu are the dwindling remains of a population once widely spread over Northern Asia, and their culture was always much like Stone Age Man's, with the addition of an animistic form of religion.

Roughly two thousand miles lie between Hokkaido and the Bering Straits by rounding the islands and skirting the coast of Kamchatka in the Bering Sea. A body could perhaps have drifted, and at long last reached the Bering Straits to become icebound there.

So an aboriginal of Ainu ancestry, victim of an attack in his own wild environment could be the remotely possible answer to the Iceman riddle, dismissing the propounded theory that the find might have once been a pre-historic man.

The Ainu type is very hirsute and primitive in spite of what was known as Caucasoid features, and their organised social system is where animism, magic, and ritual are interwoven. They might have been a distant link with the Almas near-hominid

119

type, in view of the *Ainu* race having been relics of very old human stock. Possibly, geographical and climatic circumstances advanced their evolution to the primitive level of culture that it reached, while the *Almas*, conditioned by their savage and inclement backgrounds, were forced to remain as wanderers across deserts and forests and wherever food and shelter happened to be obtainable. So their species hid in animal-like lairs and fastnesses, emerging only to raid and forage, and they never progressed to full hominid stature.

The Manchurian candidate with his wolf association, is, to my mind the most definite alien in the collection. That so-called 'man-beast' had the attributes of a real if very repulsive specimen of *homo sapiens*. Something extremely low-grade and born possibly of poor degraded stock. In spite of his primitive and animal-like tendencies he was no sub-human/half-animal at all in the strict sense. The creature's history, what there was of it, suggested that he was merely a deformed and freakish sub-mental human. He represented a phenomenon that, given similar circumstances, could happen even in this age. This is where I disagree with Dr Porshnev's opinion for the facts before me suggest the Manchurian specimen might have established wolf contacts in infancy and was probably abandoned by low-type nomads because of his freak birth. The forest beasts with their protective instinct for something young, alive, and helpless, might have been the creature's foster-parents. This has been known to happen. A case in point occurred in the Celebes Islands in 1963. A village guard near Parepare in the South Celebes, caught sight of an ape dashing through jungle carrying a human child. Police gave chase, and it dropped the child and scuttled away. After rescue the three-year-old boy behaved like an ape, only eating fruit and refusing rice. Later the boy improved under care, and was taught to talk.

The Manchurian wild man might have been a similar case. He retained his established familiarity with the wolves, and so had acquired his savagely inhuman knack of hunting and eating from continued contact with them.

The manner in which he called to the wolves, and their curious

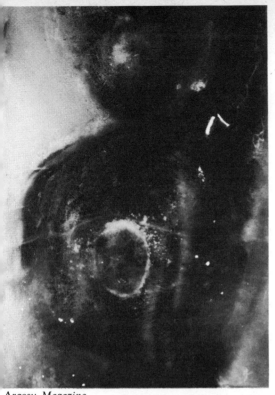

Top left, a photograph of the torso and face of the Iceman. *Top right*, an artist's drawing of the Iceman.

Left, a still from the movie taken of California's *Bigfoot*.

X marks the spot where the skull was found in the Altai Mountains in Mongolia in 1953.

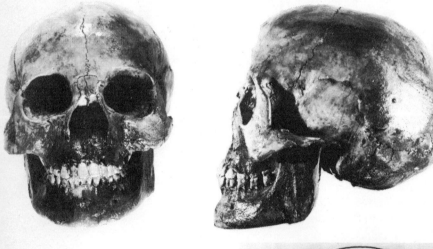

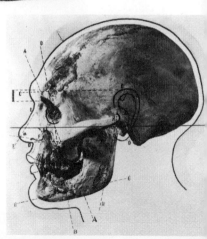

The skull as it was found, and *right*, measurements and calculations before reconstruction.

response of loping up and cautiously sitting down at first and watching him before he disappeared with them into the forest, was a truthful and non-exaggerated description.

Some years ago I had to go and see an amateur zoologist. This elderly man had effected the strangest and most genuine relationship with a pack of wolves. While waiting for our interview, not on the edge of a forest, but safely outside an open-air enclosure in which his wolf friends were penned, I experimented by talking softly to them as they circled round and round in their playground. At first they took no notice, but then a small group detached themselves from the rest, and coming right up to the rail where I stood, they sat down on their haunches and surveyed me intently out of unblinking yellow eyes. Just as those forest wolves in Manchuria had sat down and summed up their wild pal before accepting his presence.

I am sure the Manchurian "man-beast" was no animal and neither was he related to the *Almas*. Strangely enough, his sad and debased humanity repelled me far more than any *Almas* revelations.

The *Almas* are the most important on my list lined up again for speculation and comparison, although there is not much to add to what has already been recorded. According to Professor Rinchen they seem to be vanishing in Mongolia as civilisation shrinks the world and probes more and more into their old nomadic grounds. But their specifications still link up with the current discoveries of Professor Kofman in the Caucasus belt of her research. Their attributes have similarities too with the stories of the *Almas* or Snowmen of Tibet, and with the sightings and behaviour of the "wild men" of the Pamirs recorded by A. G. Pronin and others; the whole situation analysed so logically and with such clarity and precision by Dr Boris Porshnev.

The last re-assessment consists of three reports from my collection of evidence so far.

They are: the extraordinary experience of Angus McDonald in East Africa many years ago when he was attacked one night in his sleeping quarters by a mysterious brand of bogey, the *Chemosit*. Why this mystery near-candidate must be included

121

is because it displayed the now well-known Snowman characteristics of the high whining cry, musty odour, and especially the
bi-pedal walk.

The next creature to include is the *Ngoloko*, whose story was
revived by Colonel B. G. Lynn-Allen. Both these candidates appear in Chapter Nine. The mysterious *Ngoloko* had some primitive hominid attributes and was very hairy like the *Almas*. But
it had giant proportions and the dead specimen seen by African
hunters had other features of a puzzling nature for comparison. One wonders if the African tribesmen's descriptions of the
monster-like one finger and hooked thumbnail on the hands and
equally startling feet, and the enormous ears, were imaginary
impressions, exaggerations, or genuine language mistakes when
describing the encounter to white settlers. But the fact remains,
according to the story, the rather horrifying mystery species was
a bi-ped, neither ape, nor feline, just as the tall being a friend of
Colonel Lynn-Allen saw on an occasion, in uninhabited terrain
near Lake Beringo, was a live being that walked on two legs, and
described by the white hunter's tracker as "not human".

So which is which? What species ties up in relation to what,
with perhaps a gap of thousands of miles between the areas of
distribution?

The Himalayan, Bhutanese, Chinese, Russian, Mongolian and
Tibetan records are the most closely connected. Possibly each
type has its varied appearances and physical differences, just as
occurs in all humans and animals. But the species meet on certain
general points. And this holds whether we are dealing with
Anthropology or Zoology, or a vexed and still inadmissable
meeting-place between the two.

Candidates on the outer perimeter, so to speak, are the African
ones. The Link is there, nonetheless, though fraught with blank
spaces, and they cannot be dismissed from the scene.

The fringe cases are the Californian Bigfoot report and film,
and the Iceman discovery with its macabre-comic undertones.

And as for the Manchurian wild man, he can be dismissed, I
think, as an unfortunate sub-human freak, but still a human
being.

122

CHAPTER SIXTEEN

Feuds and Labels

Feuds have always existed to slow down activity in fields of progress, and rivalries in achievements and opinion can often create the most absurd and pig-headed campaigns and near-persecutions.

Years can elapse before some daring spirit's statement ceases to be a foolhardy and romantic delusion and the discovery over which he was derided for years suddenly becomes proved fact. Skeletal or fossil remains are found to substantiate a theory when the solitary forward-thinking original exponent had only been able to provide very good clues and deductions. After the new factual discovery is put to every test imaginable, the former dissentents decide that "So-and-So was right after all, poor chap. Pity he did not live to see himself vindicated." Those words are not attributed to be the utterance of any one particular dissentent. They merely epitomise an outlook that operates by and large in the exemplary set out.

The African Okapi was ignored at first, so was the existence of the pigmy hippopotamus. The Coelacanth with its spectacular four fins, was declared extinct, until that extremely ugly fish was rediscovered in 1938, and found again in the seas off Madagascar in the early 1950's.

Even the gorilla was alleged to be mythical until it was proved to be one of the great apes, and very much alive, in 1846.

*Mythical Monsters** is probably an unknown or long-forgotten book to the layman reader who has neither time nor necessity to delve into archaic literary curiosities. The author of this work, Charles Gould, B.A., spoke not only of legendary creatures, but of other species of nature that were considered myths, until in

* Published in 1886 by W. H. Allen & Co., who were then publishers to the India Office.

later years they were recognised by naturalists. On page nine Mr Gould wrote: "Madame Meriam was accused of deliberate falsehood in reference to her description of a bird-eating spider nearly two hundred years ago. Since then reliable observers have confirmed it in regard to South America, India and elsewhere."

Audubon, the great French-American naturalist and ornithologist, "was also accused by botanists of having invented the yellow water-lily which figures in a book of his called *Birds of The South*. For years he suffered that accusation, and then the truth of his words was confirmed by the discovery of the long-lost flower in Florida by a Mrs Trent in the summer of 1878."

To descend to the modern scene, controversy eddied around Dr L. S. B. Leakey and his team when they kept turning up new samples of primitive man, in the Olduvai Gorge in East Africa. For many years Dr Leakey's work has been notable in scientific circles, but even so his claims were at times disputed. These claims propounded that not only ape-man, known as *Australopithecus*, populated Africa over one million years ago, but that a real primitive man was living alongside the ape-men in the Gorge, and the doctor and his team believed that this very ancient hominid used elementary stone tools. They considered that contrary to having a tacit understanding to live and let live with his near-ape neighbour, known as the species *Zinjanthropus*, he sometimes killed and ate him.

This theory was challenged by leading authorities, but considered by others. Perhaps the cannibalism theory is debatable. *Homo Habilis*, as Leakey called his new primitive man, might have thought twice about it in view of the considerable size of his "next door neighbour", and instead go after smaller prey.

The conventional divisions of races and the labels of zoology comprise a vast monument. It has been so firmly constructed and established in the annals of the natural sciences, that any tentative alteration of terms, or revolutionary suggestion that there might be half-way houses between the divisions, is taboo.

We know that man's separate labels are Nordic, Alpine, Mediterranean, Mongolian, Negroid, and Australian (meaning the aboriginals of Australia's Northern Territory).

We know that Nordic, Alpine and Mediterranean were sometimes grouped together under the label of Caucasian. That was
because about two hundred years ago a German anthropologist
called Blumenbach gave that name to a female skull discovered
in Georgia in the Caucasus. The even older branch of a similar
type was more anciently labelled as Caucasoid, and was said to
have had connotations with the *Ainu* race.

We are aware that the simian creatures are roughly divided
into the monkeys of various species, and the anthropoidal tail-
less great apes.

Most people have a vague idea that Paleolography describes
the study of ancient writings or inscriptions; that Paleontology
is the study of extinct but once organised beings, and that in the
Neolithic age some of the human race had begun to use ground
or polished stone weapons. But nowhere can one find a small,
condensed, yet complete study in print that bridges these various
natural sciences and shows the relationship between them. This
relationship could contain references and even clues to research
which would make such a written work valuable. I am not saying that the references do not exist. They do but in diffuse form.
Generally, they can only be found under the aegis of each one
being a vast separate specialist study. And even that is frequently
presented in disseminated form.

Thus much time can be spent in searching for answers in huge
divided continents of print, coming between the investigation
and discovery in the actual physical field.

Perhaps the world mythologies are responsible for reluctance
to examine anything unexpected and out of the way unless there
is a specimen in a museum or laboratory to make it an accom-
plished fact.

Serious qualified persons and the collective human element of
establishments are afraid of making mistakes and appearing
ridiculous. So it is safer to remain on the already marked-out
guide-lines. Nonetheless, mythology and folk-history (they are
somewhat similar) are fascinating and rewarding factors, especially in the frequent very early truth-elements that began a
myth's career down the ages. Yet these histories are so full of

the fabulous and unreal that any mystery presented, having the slightest resemblance to any plausible premise, is suspect among the adherents of respectable traditional knowledge.

Loch Ness and its underwater living mystery is another illustration. The Monster became world news in 1933 and the rumours from Scotland persisted. Some amphibian remnant of pre-history existed in the dark and excessively deep waters of the Loch with its access to the sea. Rumours continued for so long that even then some quarters thought that an official study of the mystery would follow. But though sporadic investigations on the spot were mounted, nothing on a really organised scientific scale took place. Probably the joke element, as with the Californian Snowman riddle, prevented serious sustained work.

And yet, in between the nonsense stories, and one or more publicity tricks, there has beeen and still is continuous consistent evidence of something alive and unusual in the Loch. Witnesses were and are people of integrity who have lived in the locality all their lives, and have no axe to grind by making the assertions they do.

A few years ago, Mrs Constance Whyte, a long-standing and highly knowledgeable lochside resident, wrote her remarkable book "More Than a Legend". It is the most complete record of all the sightings and photographs of the monster and she has marshalled impressive chronological evidence, not only of sightings by well-known and respected inhabitants and visitors, but also factual stories of the Loch's history and the notable people of the neighbourhood. For years they had always known of this strange phenomenon and could bring personal evidence to bear on the question. Two other convincing books on the subject are "The Loch Ness Monster" and "The Leviathans"* by Tim Dinsdale, published in 1961 and 1968. He has filmed sightings on Loch Ness and shown his findings on BBC Television. Yet another book is "The Great Orm of Loch Ness"† by F. W. Holliday.

Obviously, whatever it is that inhabits the Loch it is not one

* Both Tim Dinsdale books published by Routledge and Kegan Paul, 1961 and 1968.

† F. W. Holliday book, published by Faber and Faber, 1968.

creature alone. One single living entity could not have sustained those repeated stories for so many generations. The reports date much farther back than 1933.

The creature must be breeding in the depths of the Loch, probably circulating not only in the Loch itself but in and out of the long neck of its waters forming an outlet to the open sea.

In the history of the Western Isles, and among the crofters and fishermen, the creature of Loch Ness is no novelty of the twentieth century. There are many reports dating far back in the chronicles.

There again, ridicule has been poured on the few qualified men who have dared suggest that basis existed for the stories about Loch Ness and its monster.

At the time of writing this, a new, yet long-organised, scientific search is taking place on and around Loch Ness to attempt to identify the nature of the creature.

The investigations may not dredge up the live proof, but even if they do not succeed right away, that does not imply that the long-circulating stories are holiday inventions to boost trade, or that the monster is only a large eel, or the magnified imaginings of a few eccentrics or cranks.

Just as the long delay in attaching definite identities to the vexed and mixed Snowman mystery with its varied names, does not imply that this blank space in the history of man, sub-man, and animal is an invention either.

Surely it is non-progressive to banish certain experts' experimental thoughts on study and research for the only reason that the premises in question are not yet ratified by established material proof, and subsequent dictum? Just because of the trial-error nature of a first breakthrough? Nothing authoritative on any question can ensue until first steps are taken to encourage searchings and then establish fact. Why should a more unconventional scientist be intellectually ostracised, professionally persecuted as an unsound "maverick" because he is far-seeing enough not to dismiss an unusual and daring report until the discovery or surmise is examined from all angles?

Obviously, opinion in a primary stage is not qualified to be immediately accepted, but it should not be rejected out of hand because it does not appear to fit into an accepted order.

The worst thing that can happen to a new theory is when its advancement is halted by placing it "on the table", whether it deals with anthropology, zoology, or any other of the natural sciences. The chances are that short of almost physical assault by its exasperated protagonist, it will end by being kicked comfortably *under* the table by the powers of the respectable and safe *status quo*.

CHAPTER SEVENTEEN

Beginning of Full Circle

The early parts of the final texts of Boris Porshnev's full Snowman records reveal the Caucasian discoveries. Its final chapters
return to the Russian scene.

Much of the data is unknown in the rest of the world; some of
it was found in old, ignored archives by Dr Porshnev and his
Snowman Commission of enquiry, which seems to have been the
Cinderella of Russia's official science departments.

These new Porshnev records cover the 1969 additions about
his and his colleagues' researches, travels, and endeavours to un-
ravel the mystery, and to break down the silences that have operated in nearly every country where Snowman, pre-hominid
indications appeared.

Some of the stories may seem like near-repetitions of reports
already quoted in the body of this book, but each one is important in linking together a conspiratorial web of mankind's
strange making.

Here are the most relevant excerpts.

Even in his final surveys on the Snowman-Hominid question,
Doctor Porshnev harks back to the views of Linnaeus who, in his
generation, appealed to his contemporaries and to future generations, to make a proper study of what the Russians now call the
Troglodyte species of primitive man. Linnaeus said that if the
lives of monkeys and apes aroused the curiosity that they did
among scientists, then it was totally amazing that not a single
man of science was ever prepared to discuss with him those
Troglodyte species that were so extremely similar to the *Homo
Sapiens* species. [This comment is paraphrased from the 1777
Russian translation of Linnaeus's statement].

Porshnev describes how in 1958 in the Pamirs he met Anna

Rozenfeld, an anthropologist. She and her husband said they had met there Kirghiz and Tadjik tribesmen who spoke to them of the "wild men", the creatures who, according to area, are known as the *Gulbiyavan* or *Adam-Dzhapais*, to quote only two of their names. Two previous experienced travellers, A. L. Grunberg and V. L. Bianki, had found similar reports, including legends, about the same wild men. Anna said that the various names these *Almas* were given in the wide regions she and her husband had explored were, in addition to the two already quoted above, *Almast, Dzhez-Tyrmak, Adzhina, Dev, Pare,* or *Peri,* and *Farishta.*

It is curious to note the term, *Peri.* A well-known term in other languages than Russian, it once derived from a Persian myth. It is said to describe a good fairy, a beautiful or gracious being, but originally it meant an evil genius.

In Sukhumi, a famous beauty resort on the Black Sea, an aged anthropologist, S. D. Inal-Ip, told Dr Porshnev that one name he had heard used to describe the *Almas* was "Abanauayu," or "Forest Man".

A seventeenth-century Russian manuscript speaks of a "bear-man" caught in a forest in Poland. The creature had no speech, only a roar. It was shaggy and a tree climber. In the year 1661 in forests of Lithuania some soldiers were acting as beaters and they flushed out one of these bear-men and caught him. He was sent to Warsaw as a present to King Jan Kasimir II of Poland, whose wife tried to educate the captive who never learnt anything more than a few kitchen duties.

"From the eighteenth century there was much written about this case," Dr Porshnev states. "Today, with our fresh knowledge, we can say that almost certainly this specimen was one of the old relics of Hominid primitive species, and not, as was believed at various times, merely a man who as a child had been caught and brought up by animals.

"Natives of the Pamirs once told the Russian general, Ratov, that the regions where the wild men or *Gul'biyavans* are found most commonly in more current times, are in the wild mountains of the Chinese Province of Sinkiang, that is, Chinese Turkestan, lying to the south of the city of Tashkurgan and also on the upper waters of the river Raskem Darya. Here, since time immemorial the wild man has been hunted and caught.

"A tenth-century Arab writer, Makdisi, lived in Western Afghanistan, on the caravan route to India. He once referred to the *Nasnas*, a term which even today is still used among the Tadjik tribesmen to describe the "Wild man". Makdisi wrote: 'One species of *Nasnas* is found in the Pamirs, and in desert regions between Kashmir, Tibet, and China. They are beast-like men, covered, except on the face, with hair. They leap like gazelles. Many people of those regions told me that they hunt these creatures and eat them.'

"And now, in the present, Kirghiz tribesmen in the Pamirs who have come from that particular part of Afghanistan report that the region still contains not only wild yaks, but also these wild men; mute, hairy, two-legged, living on roots, plants, and fruit."

It is inconceivable to minds attuned to civilisation to learn that these creatures' flesh is still considered eatable in some regions, and that they are hunted with the aid of dogs, or snared in traps baited with apples. Nonetheless, in one region around Kulanaryka, there is a local edict in force forbidding people to shoot them.

Not very long ago Russian troops were in the Tashkurgan area of far-western Sinkiang, close to the Pamirs. They met some of the wild men who had no articulate speech and the soldiers used to leave food out for them on the ground.

According to Dr Porshnev: "Professor B. A. Fedorovich who was in Sinkiang Province in 1959, questioned many people around Tashkurgan. There the wild men were known as the *Yaboy-Adam*; *Yavo-Khal'g*; or *Yabalyk-Adam*. They were found near the Kashmir-Pamirs-Sinkiang frontier. Wild men had also been glimpsed by hunters during the last twenty-five years in the ranges of Pakistan as well as Afghanistan.

"While a former member of the Soviet Militia, Mattuk

Abderaim, was visiting his uncle south of Tashkurgan, the uncle hunted and brought home a freshly killed *Yavo-Khal'g*. Mattuk knowing from books about monkeys and apes, said later how this specimen was far more manlike in spite of its yellowish body hair. The feet were broader than a man's, and the thumb much closer to the fingers than in the normal human hand. Mattuk's uncle told him of the extreme goat-like agility of such a creature, and how often it would turn round to face its pursuers emitting guttural cries."

Once more fear of ridicule seemed to have prevented further enquiries.

Doctor Porshnev says: "The head of an expedition, of which Professor Fedorovich was a member, prevented him from continuing his enquiries into the subject, and turned the whole topic into a joke, commenting that 'the *Yabalyk-Adam* knows his political geography, for he escapes from his pursuers into the frontier zone where he knows that shooting is forbidden anyhow!'"

In spite of continuous, sober reports by local people with no axes to grind, those reports are passed on, come to rest in official records, and there they rest without attempts being made to rationalise the situation of these strange sporadic distributions of unacceptable living beings.

Chinese notes on the creature which for simplicity of terms in these appendices I shall refer to as the *Almas*, have certain physical traits, such as moulting in April, and the knack of picking up comparatively large rocks and hurling them a good distance. Through Chinese sources came a curious account of a Pamir Kirghiz named Dubin Dostobaev, born in Chinese Sinkiang. He remembered how in or around 1912 a wild man was captured in the mountains by hunters, and was lashed on the back of a yak and brought into the village where he was fed on raw meat. Chinese authorities sent a report about him to Tashkurgan, and knowledgeable persons there took to horse and cart,

132

thanked the hunters when they arrived in the village, gave them money, and took the wild man away. No conclusion to that incident was ever available.

These hunts and occasional captures were not uncommon, and a few cases could also be discovered in the Province of Yünnan in South-West China. Educated and responsible Chinese people told K. N. Chekanov, a Russian cultural official, how, even in 1954, the Yünnan mountains harboured beings like men, but with no clothes, no speech, and living like animals.

From the mountains of South Kazakhstan and the North-West foothills of the Talass Alatau Mountains the local Kazakhs tell stories of the *Almas*, whom they call the "*Kiik-Adams*"—yet another name. Here is the same image of the totally wild creature with short body hair, unclothed, speechless, and living on whatever flesh he can find, hunt, and kill, or on various fruit and roots. Quoting one of his informants, a forest warden called Temirali Borybaev, Dr Porshnev says these *Almas* are noted for the secrecy of their existence rather than for any fierceness. He continues:

"Borybaev said that the earliest reports he had heard had come from a close friend of his own father, one Sakal-Mergan, who died at an advanced age in the 1920's. This man had met a *Kiik-Adam* as long ago as the 1870's or 1880's, the period of the Prjevalsky expedition. When hunting high up near the head waters of the Ul'ken-Akon River in the mountains, Sakal-Mergen saw a creature, bending down and then straightening up. Creeping closer behind the rocks he saw the *Almas's* body fur, greyish and pale straw colour, and that the being was quite tall, with powerful muscles. He was cleaning off some earth from some plucked roots, and eating them.

"The watcher shot at the creature, aiming at the foot. The wounded *Almas* yelled in human fashion, exactly like a man, sat down to lick his foot, and whimpered. He made off, limping rather badly, and disappeared among the rocks. The hunter trailed him for a time, and then lost track.

"Sighting reports have also come from Kazakhstan's

133

western regions along the river Volga, from the steppes in the Akmolinsk and Karaganda areas, and even from the Southern Urals. Some Chinese Moslems (Tungans from Sinkiang) live in Kazakhstan, and there they call the wild man the 'Hairy One'."

Mention of the Altyn Tagh and the Nan Shan Ranges is made here. Prjevalsky got his first reports of the man-beast in this region. A Chinese professor, Mr T. K. Shou, told Dr Porshnev and his party of a wild man spotted by a Chinese officer on the borders of Kansu and Ch'inghai provinces, and who fled with speed when followed. The officer had persistently asked the relevant authorities to mount a scientific investigation, but to no avail. In 1957 local evidence was confirmed, and people of the Nan Shan Massif stated that the Almas, was still extant there.

The Chinese put in some intelligent research from time to time, but with no results to interest official quarters in what existed in their territories. One Almas capture in 1947 ended in the captive dying, and the skin being sent to a Buddhist temple. In the Shensi Province of China came reports from responsible people who had seen live specimens of the being called in that part of the country the "Jen-Hsiung" (Man-bear), or they had seen skins. One odd feature in that area was the reputation the Almas had of being speechless and yet being able to laugh. Made in good faith, this could have been a mistake. Some living creatures, even quadrupeds, make sounds that do resemble laughter. A Chinese scholar described how, in 1954, a Hairy man was caught through his curiosity being aroused by the bait—a piece of red cloth.

In past times according to Dr Porshnev, they used to be hunted on a large scale. Some were tamed and domesticated, and trained in simple household duties as slaves. They also acted as herdsmen. A curious development since, in their own habitat in the mountains, they lived simply, like animals, having no tools or covering, and subsisting on raw flesh and wild fruit. In his revelations, Doctor Porshnev added how a Chinese professor, Hou Pai-Lou, refused to equate the Hairy man of his country with the Snow-

134

man of the Himalaya. In his view, this species, of which he had cognisance, are simply the wild descendants of an ancient tribe of people driven off into the mountains 3000 years ago. This is a rather divergent opinion.

In Chinese there is the obsolete term, *Hsing-Hsing*, meaning an ape, or the current term, *Jen-Hsiung*, ("Man-Bear"). It is only since 1950 that the Chinese began to hear about the Abominable Snowman in the Himalaya although there is a national consciousness of the *Mi-Gö*, Yeti, or *Almas* in Tibet, Sinkiang, Mongolia, the Pamirs, Bhutan, and Nepal respectively, to which three names one can add the other well-known titles of *Metch-Kangmi*, *Dremo*, *Rakshasa*—all pointing to the same image. But it is important to note that there is no folk memory or tradition alive in China about the Snowman. It was for this reason that as previously related they turned "Ravine of Apes" into the "Ravine of Stars" when compiling their records.

"From South-West China we come next to South-East Asia," says Dr Porshnev. "In the jungles of Laos and Cambodia, the mountainous areas of former Indo-China, French explorers and administrators had collected many reports of mystery creatures, sometimes said to be spirits and sometimes said to be living beings resembling men. In 1958, the French newspaper, *Journal d'Extrème Orient*, carried a report from a well-known hunter who had met, in the jungles of Cambodia, creatures of both sexes, some with young, and exactly like the Snowman description. They left precisely the same sort of tracks, although to him they appeared to be stone-age people. We asked for information about this of Professor Chang Hui-Lai, director of the Museum of the Democratic Republic of Vietnam. He sent us results of an enquiry in the Laos and Cambodian areas. Such human-like creatures are still known to the local populations, and in his book, *The War in the Jungles of South Vietnam*, Wilfred Burchett, an Englishman, included details of a *fauna still disregarded by science*. Many other similar reports come from Burma, and also news of episodic sightings in Malaya.

135

"Suddenly, we got a whole lot of reports from Southern Sumatra's tropical forest regions. Some were old accounts telling us that relic Palaeonthropoids had survived along with the rhinoceros. These pachyderms did not die by predators, but usually through being trapped in the swamps. When this happened their flesh was eaten by two-legged beings known in Sumatra as *Orang Pendek*, *Sedapa*, or *Sindai*. In recent years such creatures were gradually dying out, but Dutch hunters of the past left descriptions of several staggering encounters with them, and in the museums are sketches and casts of their footprints."

This reference to the *Orang Pendek* seems to have some connection with the story of the *Beruang Rambai* of Lord Medway's anecdote.

To the Snowman riddle Doctor Porshnev and Professor Kofman may have the ultimate answer.

CHAPTER EIGHTEEN

Half-way Through

Continuing his map-odyssey which often developed into personal expeditions, Doctor Porshnev's new documentaries now took in Eastern Siberia. *Almas* reports began in the Yablonovyy, Stanovoy, and Dzhugzhur Ranges and reports also came from Lake Baikal, northwards to the ridges of Yenisei River region, "and God knows where else among the vast expanses of Siberia. Especially to the North, you will find time and time again the same stories about these wandering man-like creatures, attracted particularly to herds of reindeer. The richest area is the Verkhoyan'e area. Here the creature was called *Chuchuna, Kuchena, Mulena,* and *Abasy* in turn. Stories tell how they appeared in the summer months, settling in somewhere along the Chukotke River."

Below is a condensed report gathered along the Lower Lena River by A. P. Okladnikov, an archaeologist, and obtained by Dr Porshnev.

"The Chuchuna are a tribe of half-men, half-animal beings, still occasionally met with in the North. The creatures have no neck and heads that consequently seem to sprout straight up from their torsos. They usually appear at night, unexpectedly, and throw rocks on the sleeping humans from the cliffs. They are given to trapping reindeer. A Yakut hunter named Makarov said he found caves inhabited by the creature on the River Lena's right bank and as far as Lake Stolb. In these lairs were many antlers, and some hides of the reindeer that had been eaten."

The following is also based on long past observations, described ironically by Doctor Porshnev in the light of previous fact-evading as "another memorandum having no scientific significance". He came across it by chance:

"In 1912 P. L. Dravert, a young mineralogist, published reports of wild hairy beings who were incapable of articulate speech, that he had witnessed, since 1908, along the Lower Lena. Later when Meteorites were his expert subject, and he had gained a professorship, he reverted to his early studies, and in 1933 published a long paper, *The Mulen and Chuchuna Wild Men*. It was a pity that this report was obscured by notes added by an unqualified assistant of his. In line with the long-established principle of denial, a refutation was levelled at Dravert by G. Ksenofontov, who wrote, 'The *Mulen and Chuchuna* are too much like the Pans and fauns of the old Greek myths'.

"Once more," says Porshnev, "the lid of the sarcophagus slams down upon an incredible truth . . ."

Yet further pointers at that time led to the Chukotskiy Peninsula and the Aleutian Islands. One Yakut tribesman assured Dravert that the hairy *Chuchuna* sometimes crossed over from the Lower Lena to the "Warm Islands", meaning the Aleutians. The Yakut told how one of them was found lying on the seashore, and it was impossible to tell if he was dead or alive, and nobody dared touch the body, even the dogs fearing to approach. He lay as dead all day. When night fell, only one tribesman, the community's Shaman, came near enough to see the creature rise from the ground and make off.

"In addition to humans passing across the Bering Straits, probably in far-off times, across a land-bridge or ice, Neanderthalers too crossed over to the American Continent via the Aleutians," Porshnev suggests. "At one time the anthropologist, Alex Hrdlicka was amazed to find complete Neanderthal-like skulls in the Nebraska *Loess*, a strata of a geological period during which, so it had been theorised, Neanderthal Man had long become extinct.

"It was in 1958 that tireless zoologist, Ivan Sanderson, began to collect American analogies to the Himalayan Snowman, the same year that we too started out on our own systematic work on the problem in the USSR. Sanderson, too, was discovering a submerged and derided prehistoric past in his own country."

It is interesting to discover the curious coincidence of several people exploring at the same time on the same theme thousands of miles apart without knowing what the others were doing, and yet all arriving at the same stage in the enquiry. At the time I too was on the same search, two years before the publication of my first Snowman findings.

Yet, as Porshnev reminds us, a hundred years ago newspapers and the diaries of travellers were full of derisive reports of wild and hairy men seen in the Canadian and Northern Californian forest and mountainous wildernesses, and partly based on stories deriving from the Red Indians and Eskimos. "The reports have continued persistently down southwards even, in Guatemala, Ecuador, Columbia, and Guyana, even since not only Sanderson, but the late Tom Slick and Victor Birn in 1960 switched attention to the Californian investigations."

Incidentally, the Californian story has flared up in every decade since the mystery was first bruited abroad, and that is the story where there might be justification for "sitting on the fence". But, as Porshnev points out: "As regards Ivan Sanderson, six of the chapters of his volume *The Abominable Snowman, Man's Ancestor in Five Continents* are devoted to summaries of American reports. Sanderson holds on to his theory that prehistoric hominid relic man is present in the New World. His book," Porshnev states, "has had no effect on the public. People avoid it and shrug their shoulders. It is dynamite but it has not exploded."

Sanderson has been criticised for his disrespect for established ideas and there was controversy too over his challenge as to whether the Holy Scriptures or Darwin were right.

139

Taking a look at a poem by Rudyard Kipling might not be amiss here: *There are nine and ninety ways of composing tribal lays, and every single one of them is right.*

Referring to the Californian sightings and film, Porshnev says:

"Evidence is there, but it will not break down stubbornness. Photographs can be dismissed sceptically and plaster casts of footprints too, and even when a species is actually caught, it will still be possible to argue that one single fact is not proof. They will say that there have always been freaks, and sports of nature.

"But from another angle, neither one single photograph, nor one single film, nor one single captured Bigfoot or his skin and bones could tell all that we have already accumulated, bit by bit about the existence of this creature all over the world."

The next evidence concerns his expedition to the foothills of the Chatkal Range in the T'ien Shan Mountains. In the vicinity lies a dark green lake called Sary Chelek. He went there in the autumn of 1959, one year after intensifying Snowman research was going on in two continents and the trip was to pursue new information.

"An engineer, and geologist, A. P. Agafonov, sent a report to our Commission for Snowman Research, and that report remained mysteriously unexplored for ten years until it eventually reached me. Agafonov was sitting in the yurt of a Kazakh herdsman on the shores of Lake Sary Chelek. Mad'yer, the herdsman, was well over eighty and blind, but quite a repository of his own clan's and neighbouring traditions and he described how his own grandfather, returning home with a young wife, rescued her a few moments later from the arms of an enormous ape-like man, or man-like ape, who was carrying her off. The husband, known as a mighty warrior in those far-off days, killed the creature with his hunting knife.

"Agafonov, as an enlightened man, explained to the yurt full of Mad'yer's children and grandchildren, that here in the

T'ien Shan there was no such thing as man-apes." This brought smiles from the audience and an excited outburst from the old man, who stood up, took a carved casket from a large chest by the yurt wall, and shouted scornfully: 'Take a look for yourself!' And he handed the casket to the geologist.

"Within the casket lay a skilfully dried hand, covered with sparse long hairs, except for on the palm. Judging by the size and texture it could have belonged to a man-like creature but Agafonov said he was too taken aback to make a sketch or written description of the relic. But he always remembered how utterly human it was. We already knew of similar cases. Here and there, hunters have cut off hands as trophies or talismans taken from the Wild Men. But these had been mere stories. On reading this report I decided to set out for the land of Grand-Dad Mad'yer "to seek a companion to the Pangboche relic hand".

[Pangboche is the Himalayan lama temple where travellers have been shown Snowman relics, although the Western world has cast certain doubts regarding their authenticity].

"G. G. Petrovich, who had taken part in the 1958 Pamir Expedition, agreed to go with me. We assembled our gear, tents, supplies and sleeping bags and set out for the T'ien Shan, immeasurably more promising for our search than the Pamirs had been. The volume of reports from the T'ien Shan region is ten times as big."

Some Russians were sceptical about Wild Men data, one, Professor A. A. Makhovtsev, being very outspoken in his criticism, according to Dr Porshnev, who does not appear unduly worried by it. He describes how the geographer E. V. Maksimov carried out a systematic interrogation of Kirghiz herdsmen, and tells of his visit to the home of the geologist M. A. Stronin who gave him of his experiences in the T'ien Shan Mountains. Stronin, with two Kirghiz guides and a groom spent a night on an Alpine meadow in a valley near the river Inyl'chek, a wholly uninhabited area even devoid of animal herds, and how at dawn the *Kirghizes* woke him in some alarm. Stronin dimly saw a shape trying to steal their horses in the valley near by and thinking the intruder an ordinary thief, shouted to him in Kirghiz to stop. Rifle in hand, Stronin rushed to the group to see the visitant was unusual though bi-pedal, with arms longer than is normal, and covered with hair. The creature slouched away and then ran quickly off. It rushed down an incredibly steep slope, and Stronin was able to see that its face was round, and not snout-like. At first he had thought the marauder was a bear. 'I have hunted many animals, but never one like that,' said Stronin. With its thick yellowish hair, it was not a human, and not an animal either.'

"Stronin's Kirghiz guides and groom were sitting on a rocky spur when he rejoined them. They were very frightened, and kept repeating that it had been a *Kiik-Kish* (another local name for the Wild Man). They flatly refused to accompany Stronin any farther.

"Stronin later had asked the biologists at the Kirghiz Academy of Sciences in Frunze, the capital city, about his encounter in the T'ien Shan Mountains. They told him that there *was* such a creature. 'Ask any Kirghiz,' one professor said.

"And 'such a creature' is still there, living, feeding, breeding in those vast expanses of the T'ien Shan Mountains. Other reports of sightings reached me on my way to discover Grandfather Mad'yer. In one case two young men from the town of Chirchik saw and photographed tracks of a fantastically big bare feet on the shores of a small deserted mountain lake. The tracks ran down to the water but there were no return imprints. Some immense creature had probably gone across to the other bank where there was much rock. A bee-keeper living not far from the lake was questioned and he stated that, according to hunters, there were very big tall men covered with hair that lived in the mountains far up.

"The footprint photograph was sent to Moscow for anatomical analysis, and the report appears to have equated with other descriptions indicating prehistoric Neanderthal Man. Just the track of a living Neanderthal who went quite recently to take a dip in a cool lake. There he goes, big, hairy, mute. That's the fellow. . . .

"The journey to Sary Chelek was long and often difficult. By air to Frunze, then by smaller aircraft to Dzhalalabad, and on to Kurgan, the regional capital town. From there it was still a fair way to Sary Chelek but already we had found people who had known the old shepherd and thought highly of him and all his lore. What my companions and I had thought would be the hardest part of our expedition (finding out his address) was the easiest. But we arrived too late. He had died, aged ninety-nine, only three months before, mourned by all his descendants and neighbours.

"At the local forestry commission offices we were given mountain ponies to journey on to where old Mad'yer's heir lived. He was the herdsman's adopted son, the Mullah Aytmurza Sakeev, and no doubt possessed the relic hand, although one ancient herdsman told us he was sure nothing would induce Aytmurza to show it to us. Finally we did track him down where he lived with his family and the widow of Mad'yer. We began with all the necessary advance palaver and promises and then they brought out a carved basket, inside which lay a hunter's talisman. Alas! The dried paws of a fox. The Mullah knew no more. He must have been counting on our naïveté. Later, near Tashkent, we looked up A. P. Agafonov who assured us the casket had not even been the same one. But the relic true hand must be somewhere.

"One man highly experienced in the customs of that Moslem world advised us that only highly-placed members of the Moslem hierarchy were ever able to exercise influence. Mad'yer's Mullah heir was evidently bound by religious-ethical considerations of some kind. Later, the Council of Ministers of the Uzbek Republic gave us some hope when they promised to ask the Mufti Babakhanov of the Moslem Church of Central Asia, to exert influence with Aytmurza Sakeev and exhort him to co-operate with us in our enquiries.

"A few months later, I was again in Tashkent, and I learnt that news had come from the T'ien Shan region that the Mullah did possess a dried hand which he had inherited. I had a friendly personal interview with the Mufti, but the enquiry tailed off. We never saw the hand."

So this travelling commission on proof for the Snowman continued, and then discovered another factor. Dr Porshnev's reconnaissance trip into Central Asia covered the mountainous region of Tadzhikistan from where many reports had been collected from various groups independently engaged in the same search. There he met a couple of hydro-electrical engineers, a father and son called Sinyavskiy, who had spent their lives in Central Asia, knew the several languages there and had gained local confidence.

A very strange element in the Snowman, or *Almas*, question interested them, and subsequently, Dr Porshnev.

A curative drug used to be prepared from the skin of the Wild Men. Nowadays, says the Doctor, the drug is carried principally by pilgrims to Mecca. At one time one of the sources of wealth of the Emir of Bukhara was from the sale of this costly medicine and supplies came in the form of annual dues paid to the Emirate by the population of the few valleys, where it was distilled by medicine men and quack doctors. A special official of the Beg of the Karatag Region had the job of collecting it for the Emir and a centre for these activities had been the village of Khakimi in the Karatag Valley. This valley had long been a "breeding ground" or "nursery" for Wild Men.

The name of the medicine was formed from the Iranian word *Mum*, meaning *fat, wax*, and the Tibetan word *Mi-Gö* meaning Wild Man. Hence the full term for the medicine, which was *Mu-gö*.

Extra research discloses that in the Middle Ages the Arabs used to sell similar medicine to Europe, and in Egypt the word *Mummy* came in time to imply the process of embalming. The colouring property of the preparation also gave its name to a colour, *Mummy*. It was used in the eighteenth, and the

144

nineteenth centuries by Reynolds and other artists. Known as *Asphaltum, bitumen,* or *Mummy,* it was, in fact, asphalt or bitumen. Some say it was obtained in those times by the grinding up of the bodies of embalmed mummies. One theory was that this is the reason why so few mummies remain today.

One more piece of rather gruesome data states that during the Middle Ages many mummies were ground up and eaten as medicine.

While Dr Porshnev was accumulating local reports during his reconnaissance, including several sightings of the now recognisable hairy figure in various desolate and normally inaccessible places, he continued his investigations on the "Wild Man Medicine".

In the valley of the River Karatag Darya a Russian hunter in recent years found a very young *Almas* child in a nest under some bushes. He had the wild child at his home feeding it on milk and raw meat. Eventually the child vanished. It was believed that it had been sold.

"Our voyages of discovery continued," says Porshnev. "One, in particular, was started from the village of Shakhrinaa, with just our laden donkey, driven on by our guide, Tura Boboev, followed on foot by A. I. Kazakov and the zoologist, S. A. Said-Aliev, while, I on horseback, brought up the rear. En route, we questioned local people about the 'Wild Men Medicine' and on how it used to be supplied to the Emir of Bukhara. In one village, its stately, grey-bearded Mullah even presented us with three precious samples of the potion.

"We visited, where possible, other ravines nearby though some of these had such dense vegetation that human penetration was not possible. We found that the left bank of Lake Par'yin Kul had long been reputed as the home of wild men. It was cut off from human interference by a raging mountain torrent on one side, and on the other by series of high ranges through which no passes led.

"Our supplies were running out so we could not attempt, by various side-trackings, to discover the other side of these ranges. But all along we had found first-hand evidence of *Almas* presence, and clues for studying the scientific foundations of the *Mu-Gö medicine*. In old Iranian writings I had already found that there were two sorts of this 'wild man' medicine. The same name was given to two different preparations. One of them, I was told, was made from the wild man himself, while the other, a substitute, was a substance gathered from rocks and caves.

"In our search for every kind of *Almas* factor, I was informed, by experts in folk medicine that they had never heard of the *Mu-Gö* preparations. But later on a discovery was made public and caused a passing sensation. In the mountains of Uzbekistan and Tadzhikistan a curative mineral substance had been found, and it was known as *Mu-Miyo*."

This last term is apparently also a corruption of the Tibetan *Mi-Gö*.

Doctor Porshnev states that its medicinal qualities had been experimentally proved. But he soon ascertained that to chemists and geologists it was proved to be just a variant of petroleum; a substance remotely like mineral wax, and *ozokerite*, or *ozocerite*, a well-known substance. This sort of *Mu-Miyo* was of no interest to him, but it led him towards more information about the real thing. He says: "Old manuscripts on Oriental medicine had frequently given a fuller acount of the real *Mu-Miyo* than I had realised. There are three schools of data on this. Firstly, the old Tibetan Medicine; then the Mediaeval Persian medicine; and, finally, the Arabian Medicine. In all three, the important factor was that the raw material used to be live or dead *Mi-Gö*, that is, Wild Men.

One of the results of Dr Porshnev's search and the collective detective work of his followers was a report of the capture and killing of an alleged Snowman in the Pamirs near the Afghan border. The body had been sent to the town of Dushanbe, Porshnev said, and described how he and colleagues hastened to the capital of Tadzhikistan. The body lay at the anti-plague station. "We were admitted with the usual official precautions,"

146

says Dr Porshnev, "but the thing turned out to be a big male rhesus monkey. Marks of a collar suggested it had escaped from captivity. By whom and with what object it had been released, or allowed to escape, no one knew (No infection was detected on it) but it did occur to me that perhaps somebody was hoping in this way to put an end to interest in the Snowman with the comment: 'Lo and behold! It was just a monkey after all.'

"Being present as the first expert to examine the specimen, I was able to tell the correspondents crowding around us that here was nothing special, and certainly not a Snowman. Fortunate for me, as otherwise I, too, might have become an object for mockery.

"But my Central Asia personal excursion had added to the general picture we already had, and was building up continuously. Everywhere upon the map we heard such remarks as these: 'A female and young were caught. They killed the young one, but the Mullah gave orders to release the female. . . .' 'The Mullah forbade them to kill it. . . .' 'The Mullah gave instructions to say nothing about it. . . .' We had many such reports of religious or local orders and counter-orders. The whole of our interrogatory work in the various regions strengthened the impression that we had invisible obstacles standing in our path.

"The hominid relic is encompassed with age-old superstition and superstitious fears, even a fear of mentioning it, or talking about it. In many of the vast regions we investigated, the whole matter rests upon instructions that issue from the Moslem priesthood. Twice while in Dushanbe I found evidence of the existence of books containing records of wild men, but the owners and the Mullahs rejected approaches made by my agents. One of the opposing parties went even so far as to say that, 'These infidel unbelievers must not know.'

"When we have filled in the ethnographic map the whole of the vast mass of reports regarding the existence of relic hominids, it will be seen that the regions concerned are primarily those in which one of three religions is present throughout the population: Mohammedanism, Lamaism, and Shamanism. There are also pockets of local heathen cults.

"My conclusions grow stronger as our search proceeds that, in the last few millennia and centuries, relic Neanderthal men have, generally speaking, survived only in those areas where they were under some degree of protection engendered by religion and religious beliefs. There is evidence that the controllers of the Lamaistic Church forbade by special decree any interference with the remaining Mi-Gös. Mohammedanism, while spreading and struggling against Zoroastrianism, found it a logical thing to become the guardian of the Devs. Injunctions and decrees were heaped upon the faithful relating to these beings, so closely resembling Man, with mortal and material 'souls'.

"But if religious belief, so boundlessly alien to Science, has preserved for Science, here and there upon earth, these priceless Neanderthal relics, these same religious beliefs stand at the present time as barriers blocking the path of investigation.

"I have made an appeal to the reason of the many Moslem believers in our vast country. The mystery of the hairy, mute 'Shaitans' does not belong to the foundation of Moslem religious dogma. The mystery is already solved, at least in its main outline. The time has now come to reveal to Science that knowledge that Science needs, and to deliver up to Science the ancient secret of the Orient."

CHAPTER NINETEEN

Full Circle

This could be called Dr Porshnev's final attempt, to date, to obtain recognition of the Snowman-*Almas* problem.

"The first news from the Caucasus caused a fearful turmoil. Ideas instilled by the search for the Snowman in the Himalaya were still dominant. The background image of immeasurable expanses of rock and ice predominated mentally, and now, suddenly, the Caucasus, our own tame, domesticated old Caucasus, betrampled by tourists and bespattered with health resorts and spas! Getting used to this new state of affairs meant a general shift around in thinking. Already at the time of the Pamirs Expedition in 1958, the newspaper *Komsomol'skaya Pravda*, had sent me comments from readers. It became clear from the outset of this renewed interest that people were not making any reference to my own writings about the *Almas* in Mongolia. No. They were talking about the Caucasus. Fancy such creatures existing even here!

"From Kabardinia in the Caucasus, a student and other correspondents wrote of similar reports. Even the creature's name in these mountains was the same as it had always been in far-away Mongolia and in Tadzhikistan. Our Commission asked Professor A. A. Mashkovtsev to crack this Caucasian nut for us and he buried himself in books, documents and archives, and made some reconnaissance trips in the actual field. His discoveries were the foundation for our Caucasian Odyssey."*

Doctor Porshnev's evidence continues: "Long ago, the zoo-

* This was getting near the time when Jeanne Josefovna Kofman's field work increased to include the Caucasus.

logist the late Professor Alekseevich Saturnin, renowned for his studies of the fauna of the Caucasus, had been describing six genera, sixty species, and over forty sub-species of previously unknown animals, nearly all of them vertebrates. But one species he had described only by means of a sketch, and not in an official zoological paper. He had never had a chance of examining this unknown species on his laboratory table. The title '*Biaban-Guli*' accompanies his sketch, a very similar name as heard in the Pamirs where it is '*Gul'bi'Yavan*'. This was published as long ago as 1899."†

"In the Azerbaijan region where this took place they also called the *Almas* by slightly different names. The males are sometimes known as *Guleybaney*, and the females as the *Vil'moshin'*. They would appear in the vicinity of populated settlements in the autumn, drawn there by melon fields, orchards, and gardens. But in summertime they stayed close to the great rivers that teemed with fish, frogs, and crabs. Hunters would find tracks of them later on in the winter snows. Again, investigators still found themselves up against invisible walls of silence. There is an ancient custom there forbidding local hunters to kill the wild men and according to some accounts, the minority race of the Tats (who have affinity to another little-known race called the Ossetes) may be responsible for this custom. The Tats killed the wild men at certain times and used them as sacrificial offerings for their sacred altars of pagan origin. For this very reason the Tats are all the more determined to conceal information of the hairy wild men's habitat.

"But there is one case from those parts which has not been kept secret. A Captain Belalov of the Militia in the Azerbaijan Republic, told how one of his soldiers, a simple and honest man called Ramazan, was walking home very late from duty when the moon was full. On the way to his village, after crossing a small bridge over a stream, he beheld a huge shaggy

* Professor Saturnin's encounter in the Talysh Forest from which the sketch must have been derived has already been quoted earlier on in chapter 3.

creature. It leapt at him from the shadow of the trees and carried him off to the foot of a tree, where a second figure, equally huge and hairy, a female, was standing. Both emitted strange inarticulate noises, and began to examine his face and the shiny buttons on his soldiers' tunic.

"Ramazan was so terrified he forgot that he had a revolver. But he did not faint when confronted with the two enormous wild people, man and woman, and quite naked except for thick dark hair. The female was the smaller of the two, with a bosom that lolled and dangled, and long hair on her head. Neither had facial hair, but their faces were repulsive and apelike. The soldier lay there motionless, watching them and when he tried to move the male gave a warning snarl. They then began a frightening quarrel over him. No sooner did the female touch him than the man growled and pushed her away. Then the male attacked him, and she pushed him away. At approach of dawn they made off into the forest, but it was an hour before the stunned soldier could stagger on his way home.

"He gave a full account of his adventure to the authorities, Captain Belalov told me. It was evident the man had really had that experience.

"The USSR Academy of Science's Commission on the Snowman received more than one report of such incidents, including a story of the capture of a wild man high up in the mountains of Daghestan."

But something disastrous always happened so that there could seldom follow any logical survey.

"On one occasion, V. S. Karapetyan, a Lt. Colonel in the Army Medical Service, was asked to come and examine a captured specimen. and his description equated with several others from persons who had had first-hand encounters with the creatures. But the Colonel heard nothing more. The local authorities unable to form any conclusions, had probably decided, that the specimen was a freak human and an army malingerer."

Several other confrontations, or evidence of the Wild Men occur in other parts of the Russian Republics. In certain parts of the Caucasus, they are known by yet another name, the *Kaptars*. No doubt such diversities result from the diversity of languages in the outposts of the USSR.

Doctor Porshnev states: "The first investigators who went to work on the Snowman problem in the Caucasus between 1959–1960 and onwards, combed the farther side of the main Caucasus Range, that is, the Zakatal' and Belokansk areas of the Azerbaijan Republic. One of the first prospecting expeditions was carried out by S. M. Lukomskiy, a member of the Geographical Society of the USSR and from herdsmen and others he gathered accounts of recent meetings with male and female *Kaptars*. One of the people he questioned surprised him by remarking: 'Why do you ask us all these questions when everything about the *Kaptar* is already written down and his picture shown in an Arabic book we have in our own village?' The man offered to lead the traveller to the owner of the book, probably the Mullah. But Lukomskiy did not go, for he could not understand Arabic. Anyhow, it was obvious they would not have shown him the book, as the same prejudice and secrecy towards strangers prevailed.

"Professor Yuri Ivanovich Merezhinskiy, holder of the Chair of Ethnography and Anthropology in the University of Kiev, was an unending source of information on the Caucasian relic Hominid during the first stages of our investigations, and up to his own death. With a group of students the Professor penetrated into the life of the high mountain villages, seeking out witnesses to the wild men, questioning everyone, even chance people in bazaars and on road sides. His eager searchings led to more revelations, one of which was at Belokanakh. Here he met an extremely experienced old night-hunter, who told him of his several encounters with a white *Kaptar*. This obviously referred to an albino wild man living in that region. Completely white specimens have been observed in various regions of our 'map'. It is a frequent mutation.

"Hajji Magoma, the old hunter, agreed to take Merezhinskiy with him to sit up through the night at a hide and see a *Kaptar*, but only on the express condition that the Professor

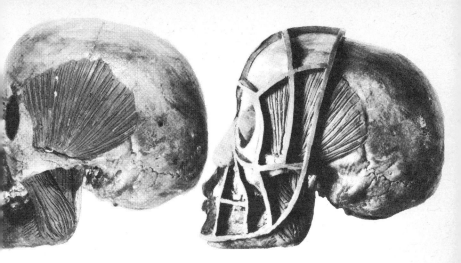

rst and second stages in the reconstruction, as combs of muscular cover are laid down.

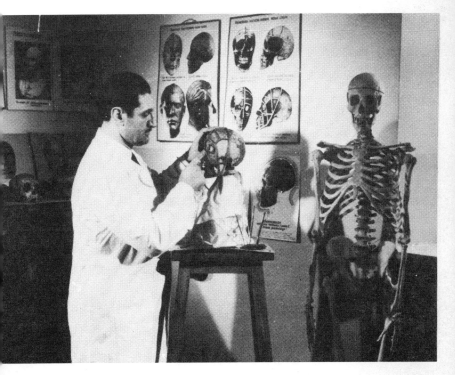

Wienczyslaw Plawinski at work.

The completed reconstruction, without hair of course.

An artist's drawing of a Neanderthal family, commissioned by the British Museum.

would photograph, but not shoot it. The hunter wanted to put to shame the many folk who did not believe his stories about white *Kaptars*.

"On the night, September 18th, 1959, there was a half moon, and Hajji Magoma led the party, which included Josefovna Kofman and one other. In addition to his camera, Merezhinskiy had concealed a revolver in his pocket, a great mistake. They went to the shrubbery-covered bank of a small stream and there the hunter and the professor crouched together, having a good view of the greensward by the stream. Miss Kofman and the other observer had their cache a few paces away.

"Quite soon, in the night silence, they heard splashing. The *Kaptar* was there bathing in the stream. He emerged on all fours on to the bank and stood up, very thin, with slender limbs, proving what variety occurs in the species. He was covered from head to foot with completely white hair, and all at once uttered sounds reminiscent of snatches of human laughter like 'he, he, he!' Hajji Magoma whispered: 'Snap him now!'

"Instead, on some impulse the professor probably could never explain the sound of a revolver shot broke out. Merezhinskiy's hands were trembling as Hajji Magoma cried, 'Why did you shoot?'

"The next sound was the noise made by the creature as, disturbed, though untouched, it made its get-away through the water.

"Running up, Josefovna Kofman found the Professor in a state of extreme agitation over his own inexplicable loss of control. Sweat was pouring down his face.

"Hajji Magoma never again took curiosity-seekers to his midnight hide.

"And subsequently the main work of questioning the populace in those regions was taken over by Miss Kofman. She was seized with a great wonder and enthusiasm, and was driven on in her search by a passion worthy of Christopher Columbus. She set forth on expeditions during three summer seasons. She climbed through villages in the valley of the River Alazan,

153

and then to the villages up on the slopes of the main Caucasus Range in Northern Azerbaijan. She learnt how to win over the taciturn mountain people and get them to talk. What she learnt included an account of how one man, an employee of a hydro-electric plant had been chased up a tree by one of the hairy men, and held prisoner for hours. The man, Lativov, had hung on, numb from fright and his unaccustomed predicament. Inexplicably, the *Almas*, tired of the waiting game, had made off.

"Little by little, the individual accounts of encounters, past, and almost contemporary, with the *Kaptar*, or the *Meshe-Adam* (another variant of the same thing) began to pile up. The outline of the new species was emerging; new in a sense, and yet old in the sporadic records of centuries. Many of the new features were surprising, and at times puzzling.

"Other men, who gained their first schooling in this fresh subject of study in the Caucasus, were Professor N. L. Burchak-Abramovich, and his assistant, F. Akhnudovy. In addition to the recording of eye-witness stories, they made sketches and plaster-casts of footprints."

Doctor Porshnev himself went to the Caucasus on a reconnaissance, and met local persons who had already given Miss Kofman and Burchak-Abramovich details of meetings with the *Kaptar* or *Almas*. One of those informants told them the now familiar story of the reluctance of people in surrounding regions to speak about the wild men owing to prevalence of religious prejudices.

Their host was a thirty-year-old carpenter, Mamed Omarovich Alibekov, who said to Miss Kofman: "I always thought the Government knew about the wild hairy men. For people have talked about this openly when they saw *Kaptars*. There was lots of chatter between ourselves. I was sure that everybody knew about them just as one knows about bears, wild boars, and even aurochs of old, and other animals. I really thought the *Kaptar* was already in museums and zoos."

Here is another attitude, illustrated when Porshnev and his party visited a well-known hunter, Gabro Eliashvili. He had already told previous guests of his experiences, and admitted that he had seen wild men while he was watching at game traps and snares. And he claimed to have shot two of them, and buried them. His son had done the same. But, "when we were guests in his house," Dr Porshnev revealed, "our gracious host replied to our question with astonishment, and said that never in his life had he heard of the pre-hominid, the wild hairy man. What was it that sealed his lips?"

In the district of Abkhazia, the Abkhazians who migrated to the region at one time, drove out the pre-hominids, whom they called the *Abnauayu.*

While collecting reports in 1962, a colleague of Porshnev, Professor A. A. Mashkovtsev, heard and studied the story of *Zana.* Subsequently, Porshnev took over where he left off.

Zana was a female abnauayu who had been caught and tamed and who lived and died within the memory of a number of people still alive today. She was buried in the village of Tkhina in the Ochamchir region in the 1880's or 1890's. Among present inhabitants of that village and district more than ten were at the funeral, and over one hundred are alive who knew Zana over a long period. A detailed account came from Lamshatsv Sabekia (aged about 105), and from his sister, Digva Sabekia, who at the time she spoke was over eighty years old. Others who spoke of Zana were Nestor Sabekia (rumoured to be 120 years old), Kuona Kukunaa, Alyksa Tsvizhba, and a person called Shamba. Of these all were alleged centenarians but there was scarcely a house in the locality where Zana was not remembered.

The manner of her capture is vague. Some said she was found in the mountain-covered forests of Zaadan. Others that this happened near the sea coast near what is today known as Adzharia. The very nickname of Zana suggests Adzharia as the spot, as it is associated with the Georgian word "Zangi" meaning dark-skinned or negroid.

Zana was not a chance catch. Hunters familiar with an age-old technique tied her up, and, when she furiously fought back, hit her with cudgels, gagged her mouth with felt, and shackled her legs to a log. Probably she had already changed hands by sale when she became the property of the ruling prince D. M. Achba who was the titular head of the Zaadan region. She passed into the possession of one of his vassals, named Kh. Chelokua and still later she was presented to a nobleman who visited the region. Edgi Genaba took her away, still shackled and chained, to his farm in the village of Tkhina on the River Mokvi, some seventy-eight miles from Sukhumi.

At first Genaba lodged her in a very strong enclosure and nobody ventured in to give her food, for she acted like a wild beast. It was thrown to her. She dug herself a hole in the ground and slept in it and for the first three years she lived in this wild state, gradually becoming tamer. After three years she was moved to a wattle-fence enclosure under an awning near the house, tethered at first, but later she was let loose to wander about. However she never went far from the place where she received her food, and she could not endure warm rooms.

Village children teased her with sticks, and she would smash the sticks in fury and chase them and domestic animals away, bombarding them with her own improvised weapons of sticks and stones.

Her skin was black, or dark brown, and her whole body covered with reddish-black hair. The hair on her head was tousled and thick, very high like a Caucasian hat known as a "Papakha". It was a black, thick shock, very shiny and hanging mane-lie down her back. She could not speak but made sounds and mutterings, and never learnt the local tongue. But she had a sharp sense of hearing, and carried out commands given by her master. She was scared when he shouted at her, a strange reaction from this massive tall creature, thick-set, with huge bosom, muscular arms and legs, and fingers that were longer and thicker than truly human fingers.

From remembered descriptions given to Doctor Porshnev, her face was terrifying; broad with high cheekbones, flat nose and eyes of a reddish tinge. Memories of her indicated that the most frightening feature was her expression which was purely animal,

156

not human. Though, one never knows why such comparisons are sometimes made to denote intimidating characteristics, for often an animal's eyes can be expressive enough to suggest human intelligence.

She lived for many years without showing change; no grey hair and no falling teeth. Her teeth were enormous and she could crack anything with them. She would outrun a horse, and swam the wild Movki River even when it rose in violent high tide. To gorge herself with grapes in the vineyards, she would pull down a whole vine growing around a tree. She loved wine, and was allowed her fill, after which she would sleep for hours in a swoon-like state.

Zana never actually attacked children but just shoo-ed them off. She was trained to perform simple domestic tasks, such as grinding grain for flour and carrying firewood. Sometimes she went into the house, but she only obeyed her master. She had a curious obsession for playing with stones, grinding them together, or smashing them. Some who watched her wondered at that urge to chip fine-pointed pebbles of the Mousterian type, as was done by Neanderthal Man whose remains, years later, were actually dug up on one of the very hills Zana used to roam.

Zana became the mother of human children. This is the fantastic side of her history, and important, according to those studying the science of Genetics. Zana was pregnant several times by various men and she gave birth without assistance, but always carried the newborn child to wash it in the cold river. The half-breed infants, unable to survive these ablutions, died.

So when subsequently Zana gave birth, the villagers began taking the newborn away from her in good time, and reared them themselves. Four times this happened, and the children, two sons and two daughters, grew up to be humans, fully-fledged and normal men and women who could talk and possessed reason. It is true that they had some strange physical and mental features, but all the same they were fully capable of engaging in work and social life.

The eldest son's name was Dzhanda, and the eldest daughter was Kodzhanar. The second daughter, Gamasa, died only forty years ago, while the younger son Khvit, died in 1954. And all of them had descendants of their own, scattered in various regions of the Abkhazian Republic.

"In 1964," says Dr Porshnev, "I visited two of Zana's grandchildren in the town of Tkvarcheli, where they work in a mine. They are a son and a daughter of Kvit by his second marriage, with a Russian woman. There are insistent rumours that the father of Gamasa and Khvit was in fact Edgi Genaba himself, but in the census they were put down under a different surname. It is significant that Zana was buried in the family cemetery of the Genabas, and that the two youngest children of Zana were brought up by Genaba's wife.

"Many local people in those parts remember Gamasa and Khvit clearly. They were both powerfully built with dark skins and rather Negroid features. But they inherited scarcely anything from Zana's Neanderthal facial appearance. The complex of human features was dominant in them, and yielded a different line of descent, so they were not hybrids. Khvit, who died at the age of sixty-five or seventy, was described by people of his home town as little different from the human norm, except for certain small divergences. He had a dark skin and thick lips, his hair was not negroid, but stiff and straight, the head small in proportion to his body. He was extremely strong, difficult to deal with and wild and turbulent. He lost his right hand after one of the many fights he had with his fellow-villagers, but his left hand sufficed him to mow and do other work on a Kolkhoz farm, and even climb trees. He had a high-pitched voice and could sing well. When old, he moved from his village to Tkvarcheli where he eventually died, but he was taken back for burial at Tkhina beside the grave of his mother, Zana.

"From the first moment I saw Zana's grandchildren, I was impressed by their dark skin and slightly negroid looks. Shalikula, the grandson, has unusually powerful jaw muscles and he can pick up a chair, with a man sitting on it, with his teeth, and he can dance. One of his gifts is imitating sounds of wild

158

and domestic animals.

"In the capital of Abkhazia I was introduced to a man I was told could help me to find the skeleton of Zana. Others had boggled at the task, fearful of offending the relatives and afraid of local Moslem traditions.

"My new contact, Vianor Pandzhevich Pachulia, is the energetic director of the Abkhazian scientific and investigatory institute of tourism. He is an enthusiast, and a champion of the antiquities of his motherland. Under his guidance in September 1964, the artist and archaeologist V. S. Orelkin and I made our first attempt to find Zana's grave. The cemetery was all overgrown and only the ten-year-old mound over Khvit's grave can be picked out among the bracken covering the hillside, where nobody else has ben buried since then.

"Zana must be somewhere near. We asked the old residents and the last scion of the Genaba clan, seventy-nine-year-old Kentoi, was clear that we should dig under a pomegranate tree. What was found there turned out to be the remains of one of Zana's grandchildren who had died early, for the profile that we established from the skull was extraordinarily like the profiles of Zana's two living grandchildren whom I myself had met."

After two more expeditions the search party had still not found Zana's bones, though in a third attempt in October 1965, they found what are probably the bones of Gamasa, as they present slight, but definite Neanderthal features. The search for Zana will continue.

"Statistics meanwhile have been piling up. Under Jeanne Kofman's direction all reports of encounters with relic Hominids, in Northern Azerbaïjan and other areas of the Caucasus, have been put on to graphs and charts, showing percentage of sightings, dates, time of day, and whether cases are adult or young, male or female. It appears that very few young ones are seen in the main Caucasus Range, and a lot less females than males. This means that it is one of their migration areas, and that the focal breeding area is elsewhere. The preliminary data assembled in the Kabardino-Balkaria Region however promises that *there* the proportions among sexes and age-groups will be quite different.

"We think Kabardinia will be a new stage, a new level, in our whole investigation. This spot on the map is the arena where field research of the Relic Neanderthal Man has been pushed further ahead than anywhere else. This Neanderthal is related to the 'Podkumskiy Man' whose remains have been excavated in just this area.

"For this, Soviet and World Science owe a debt to Jeanne Josefovna Kofman. She switched the base of her operations to Kabardinia in 1962. There is a heroic streak in her, and in this search she had found her vocation. She is a specialist of the first rank, attracting to herself, and directing the efforts of, many young workers.

"For the solution of the world-wide problem of relic hominids, Kabardinia is not the rule, but the exception. For in Kabardinia this species of creature exists unusually near the homes of men, and human settlements. Consequently, the kind of relationship with man is a very special one. Kabardinia today is a veritable anthropological laboratory and an inducement to us to solve the problem once and for all. Kabardinia was an area from which no visiting scientist or geologist had ever made any report or voiced an opinion and the workers in the fields who co-operate with us, refuse to take notice of the outside criticisms that reach us, which is often that the native population of the region are all telling lies. Why should they, the local people demand? There is no reason for it."

All the same there was at the outset an accumulated body of stories that could cause speculation.

One report told the experience of a Russian woman visitor, N. Ya. Serikova, a senior zoo-technologist, who in 1956 arrived in the Zolskiy region of Kabardinia. She had never heard local stories about the *Almas* and she lodged during her stay in the house of a collective farm worker. One evening while she was lying on her bed in her room with the house door open, letting in sounds of a wedding party celebration next door, she looked down, and: "Suddenly I hear a sort of screech, and to my horror there is a being, all hairy sitting on its haunches on the floor staring at me. Its left hand was on its right shoulder, and its right on its left. I thought by its look it was going to leap at me, and lying petrified I cried out 'Lord, where did you come from?' I am not a God-believer. The creature screeched again, and dashed off giving the door such a bang that the whole house shook. It left behind in my room a stifling sour smell. I know no smell like it. I did not get up or move till next morning. I thought it was probably something devilish."

Only next morning did she learn that the visitant was no devil, but an *Almas* that lived next door in a house that had once belonged to an old woman, now dead, who must have befriended it. The sounds of the wedding revelry had no doubt disturbed it.

I have a feeling that this is a very "fringe" anecdote, and it has a curious dream-like quality about it, a connotation with fables of monsters, phantoms and the like.

But many far more authenticated cases were collected by Miss Kofman and Dr Porshnev. One Russian bee-keeper near Mount Elbruz suffered an *Almas* raid on his apiaries. He asked his young brother, who was in the army, to come to his aid and together they caught the raider, and actually shot him dead. Another case happened when Khuker Akhaminov, a collective farm worker in Kabardinia, found two newborn baby *Almas* in a field of sunflowers. A female of the species had just given birth to them and deposited them in a grass nest while she decamped temporarily on the man's approach.

The farm worker rushed away with his horse and cart to tell his family and friends but for some reason nobody went back to the sunflower plantation until three days later. They found nothing. No doubt the mother *Almas* had returned for her progeny.

Doctor Porshnev and his party asked the farm worker: "Why did you not report the matter? The man answered: "But to whom should I report, and why?"

Porshnev says: "We told him: 'But surely you know that it

is a very interesting matter, and that scientists are studying it?'

" 'Who knows that it is necessary. . . . I never in my life heard that there was anybody that was interested in it.'

"And that probably is an accurate diagnosis of the situation," was Dr Porshnev's final comment on the incident.

There have been other cases, of Almas in ordinary human homes, apart from the experience of the woman zoological technologist and the story of Zana.

One interesting and lasting relationship occurred in Kabardinia. There have been many occasions when men have actually kept an *Almas* after capture, but the creature generally got away. The story of Khabas Kardanov was quite special. When a young man, he encountered a female *Almas* after she had been tamed by some faithful Orthodox Church believer, and then somehow had lost her protector. Many people in Kardanov's village of Sarmakovo, including his own family, knew that this female *Almas* came to his house and an uncle of Kardanov, Zamirat Legitov, once met her in his nephew's home.

Eventually friends of Kardanov persuaded him to say how this came about. A few months before, he had met this horribly hairy woman in a patch of tall weeds. He was petrified but the *Almas* woman was not; she continued to sit there. A few days later he ran into her again, and then several times more. He sometimes threw food at her, and soon was feeding her regularly. Then one day, when he had to drive a herd of cattle back to Sarmakovo, the *Almas* followed him and took up abode in his house.

He taught her a few tasks, and she was a quick and willing worker, he said, and very strong. She loaded hay on his cart with ease and in her inarticulate way she tried to please. Her efforts may have been embarrassing at times, as when she used to go off and steal tomatoes for him somewhere or other far from Sarmakovo. Kardanov said: "She knew no human language, but used to mutter things that were quite unintelligible." On one occasion, when Kardanov's uncle visited him, she came into the room with an armful of stolen tomatoes and sat down, muttering and groaning to herself.

It is of interest that the young man's parents never hid these matters, but would tell their friends. Their only concern was that they feared the *Almas* woman might bring ill fortune to their son.

At first Kardanov laughed about it, but after two or three years he worried as to how to get rid of her. It was impossible to drive the creature away.

In the spring of 1959, an engineer, M. Tembotov, was collecting *Almas* reports on behalf of his zoologist brother, A. Tembotov. Hearing about Khabas Kardanov and his dilemma, he negotiated with him. Kardanov made it clear to him that he had no objection to ridding himself of his tame but troublesome *Almas* woman, but he was, nonetheless, keeping an eye on the main chance. He was a sharp bargainer and asked a pretty penny for her.

The final climax came when Tembotov telephoned the Commission for instructions. It must be remembered that in 1959 existence of the Snowman in the Caucasus had scarcely yet established itself in the minds of the Commission Members. What is more, the Commission had only recently suffered what Dr Porshnev describes as a "Shipwreck" in the Academy of Sciences. Consequently, there was nowhere whence the Commission could obtain money to purchase the *Almas*. As a result, Tembotov had to break off negotiations with Kardanov.

Not long after, Kardanov went off to work in Siberia. Those close to him said this was due to his increasing desire to rid himself of his *Almas* woman.

What happened to her is unknown. But Kardanov's departure is certainly the most unique reason to account for exile in Siberia.

The Kabardinian field experimental station under Miss Kofman's leadership is no mere whim, according to Dr Porshnev. It is not a gamble on chance, but an unswerving forward movement. Every year, he says, brings the creature under observation nearer and nearer into view of the team of investigators. Its nature is seen more and more distinctly, each season, bringing in

163

its wake some discovery or other, something these scientists on the spot did not know before.

Nearing the conclusion of his current and latest long record, Dr Porshnev says:

"An enormous amount still remains unknown to us. The task of extracting what is general from all the eye-witnesses' accounts is not easy. The cases not only do not resemble folk-lore, they are its very opposite. The skeleton of folklore is repetition. In the dossiers of our Kabardinia field-laboratory there are no two accounts that are alike. There is neither unity of subject nor of style. In reconstructing an image, the re-searcher proceeds by processing differing reports, and not by linking the similar ones. The Palaeonthropus, incidentally, is not standardised. The *Almas*, both in outer appearance and in behaviour, is extremely individualistic. Much in each separate case is unique.

"In a single working season Miss Kofman's field group moved forward to a new objective. This is the possibility of collecting clusters of individual reports about *one and the same Almas* creature, so that it is recognisable by unquestionable signs. Various persons have noted individual characteristics in one single specimen, in places not far apart, and for brief periods of time. This is to be a new peep-hole for us into the hitherto little-known world of these elusive and shadowy creatures, and one that should bring it all much closer to us.

"In her regular report to the Soviet Geographical Society, Miss Kofman, in the spring of 1966, drew a sketch of the skull of Modern Man on the blackboard. And there, beside it, the skull of Fossil Neanderthal Man. Next to it, she drew, with the chalk transforming words into lines, the combined result of scores of records about the skull of the *Almas*. Before our eyes the outcome seemed plain. The third sketch is identical with the second.

"It is hard to say whether we are halfway yet. Our Cau-casian relic Hominid, ranging from those in the Alpine meadows around Mount Elbruz to the Kabardinian settlements down in the plains, possesses features still unsuspected by us. The reports are numerous, and yet, when all is said and done, informants are only a tiny percentage of the population of Kabardinia, and most informants have only seen an *Almas* once or twice in their lives.

"In November 1967, Miss Kofman and I accepted an invitation to speak at Pyatigorsk at a regional conference on medical geography, and from there we went to visit the Kabardian base of our field expeditions. On seeing those vast virgin expanses of valley, forest and mountain, one realises how easily it could still be the haunt of Neanderthal relics. It is only necessary to drive the *Almas* down into settled and planted lands.

"What we have gathered so far, from all over the world, are reports of *unpremeditated* encounters with the *Almas* or Snowman. The only expected encounter I know of was that of Yu. I. Merezhinskiy."

The mind strays here to that *unpremeditated* revolver shot of the erudite professor. It gives an interesting psychological sidelight on what excitement and sudden panic can trigger off at times even in the most educated and informed person.

Doctor Porshnev comments: "An old Kabardinian once said to me: 'They are here all right, but they know how to hide themselves. There could be one over there on the other side of the street and you wouldn't see it!'

"*Snowman*—a laughable term. But what hides behind the smiles is the isolation and the loneliness for the small band of his seekers.

"Why this sentence of strict isolation, when what we are seeking is so new, so important, so irrefutable that you would think thousands of hands would reach out to help us? There are a few it is true, who do reach out to assist, but each of these is still doomed to suffer the fate of being treated as something outcast for their daring to find out the truth.

"This is a struggle to reach the youthful scientists, a battle for their conscience which is the very foundation of Science.

But ranged against them are the authorities with their weapon of silence against what they forbid. I could quote many examples of this organised silence. For instance, when in 1959 leading members of the Chinese Academy of Sciences were in Moscow, they advised that their *Academy* possessed very important material they could not yet communicate, but which they would release to us by August 1960. Months went by, and at the advised date I wrote to my Chinese opposite number, the head of their commission, on the problem of the Snowman. There was no reply.

"Long afterwards came the *unofficial answer*, via a third party, that 'Professor Porshnev should not think we want to hide anything, but the material we have, as well as the question of its publication, is still under consideration by the highest authorities.' Since then, nine years have elapsed.

"In the interim [it was in 1964 actually] at the International Anthropological Congress in Moscow, there was a symposium on the fascinating theme 'The Border between Man and Animal'. The speaker was the biologist, Professor Doctor L. P. Astanin, who began, 'A few words about the so-called Snowman. . . .'

"The Chairman of the meeting was the Soviet anthropologist and biologist, Dr V. P. Yakimov. He leapt to his feet. For the first time in the whole history of international scientific congresses, a participant in the congress was driven from the rostrum.

"In vain Astanin assured him that he was only going to speak about the anatomy of the hand."

A new theory or near-discovery is almost always parried with the retort: "You catch one first!"

It would appear that the same category of sceptics once told K. E. Tsiolkovskiy, a Russian scientist of the nineteenth century when he spoke of interplanetary space rockets, "You fly to the Moon first, and then you can talk about it!"

Doctor Boris Porshnev concludes this longest section of his monumental documentaries on the search for the truth about the

Snowman with the words:

"Our next task is not to catch the *Almas*, but to photograph them; then to semi-domesticate them, and then to set up a Reserve. Only stubborn research will get us to that goal. We must endeavour to penetrate the sphere of human opposition to our search, and the sphere of biological self-defence in the natural system of the *Almas*.

"Both those defences we have already scratched. We have not penetrated them."

CHAPTER TWENTY

Round-up

While extraordinary developments have taken place at the roots of the problem, conventional searches are mounted from time to time to solve the Snowman mystery. They follow the old tried and unsuccessful pattern.

The Snowman does not live at high altitudes above the snowline even though the creatures and, more often, their tracks have been found at such heights. They were only moving from col to col, either for food, or on some mysterious search of their own.

Their habitat in the Himalaya and other similar geographical areas is in dense, uninhabited mountain forests and gorges below the snowline, and in some of the wildernesses of Central Asia and the Chinese borderland. In any case, they are rare.

The average person still thinks humorously of the Snowman (if he thinks about him at all) as a strange Himalayan product of legend and superstition, when actually the Snowman, *Almas*, *Yeti*, *Mi-Gö*, whatever his several other names, is showing himself more and more to be the forgotten link tracing patterns over much of the world, even leaving a tenuous trail of memory in Europe itself. Ancient hearsay recorded how, in the densely forested Europe of old, and its off-shore islands, "Wild Men" of the woods and the hills were known by an Anglo-Saxon term, the *Wudewas*. It has been suggested etymologically that the name *Woodhouse*, or *Wodehouse*, in Britain stemmed from just that.

Down the centuries gaps were left in the living world's history through the fetish for established fact, and through man's pride in himself as self-styled Lord of Creation, now fashionably labelled a hairless mammal—the spirit within the body dismissed.

Some unusual factor must have contributed to the "Wild Man" mystery; the existence of rough, unfinished beings described or encountered by simple people in remote places, and by others not so simple but trying to find out the truth. Something lost and forgotten in evolution caused these frightened, pathetic, and often frightening creatures to be left behind.

The Missing Link? This Anthropological question was debated, reported solved, and then faded away into the indefinite. What was the matter, when the missing links were there, sporadically sighted, disputed, but repeatedly reported?

It may have been a kind of neurosis of the centuries, this silence on living, hidden replicas of primitive ancestors. They should have died out decently as Science announced. It was an embarrassment that stone-agers scattered in impossible places did not have the tact to vanish completely.

The animals have had a better deal than these sparse, semi-concealed creatures. Animals are recognised and have their places in the echelon branches of the tree of life, but the outcasts, unacceptable elements (insisted upon as being legend) have had the temerity to live on in a few of the rare, savage places still left.

There is a belief that if a statement is made often enough it is eventually considered to be true by the majority, whether it has been proved correct or not. It proves less trouble to do so. And this is what must have happened when the stone-agers were left behind in the race to the top, sentenced by geographical and climatic conditions to remain in an elementary and awkward stage of evolution that possibly had once been ours.

On looking back down the centuries that have made us superior, one regrets this hidden dilemma of man; is this a riddle too slight in worldly opinion, too unimportant to try to solve by bringing facts to light? This could be Science's predicament.

"If they really have survived here and there, the pre-hominids will die out," cold opinion will probably predict, "It is the natural solution."

Is the Russian concept of establishing reservations a better answer, should they eventually gain the trust of those diminishing twilight creatures and gather them within their field of scientific research?

The mind boggles at the problem of attempting human approach to such primordial beings. Yet remembering Dr Porshnev and his Commission in the years-long voyages and field sessions of discovery, it is logical to surmise that the Caucasus experiments and the collaboration of fellow-experts in other parts of the world, will lead to some definite result.

The Russians have never been people to do things by halves.

A lighter side does occur to me. After I had *travelled* (there is no other word for this) page by page and report by report through Boris Porshnev's impressive monumental work (and I suppose what I have studied is only a portion of all his documentaries) I remembered another Russian epic I had heard about.

I was told the story of Serge Eisenstein, film producer and genius who made the film *Potemkin* many years ago. Later, in Mexico, when he was directing his magnificent documentary on Mexican history, the magnitude and splendour of theme and scenery exerted such a fascination upon him that he went on shooting well beyond the margin set by the Hollywood moguls. Hollywood at last urgently cabled him to stop. Though they had given him a free hand, this was getting beyond even their largesse. But Eisenstein with Russian enthusiasm retorted that the material unfolding before him was so wonderful that he could not stop just like that, and went on shooting. He got sacked and the magnificent film lay in the can for years and years. I only saw it myself a few years ago quite a long time after the 1939/1945 war.

The Porshnev records are equally marvellous in their own way, but lengthy as the accumulation of his discovery is, I am quite sure that it will not suffer the fate of the Eisenstein film that Hollywood "killed" for so many years. And I hope I have been able to do a little justice to him in my interpretation.

Some reactions to the "Wild Men" of the various country people described have their humorous moments. A smile is evoked by the logic of some of the Moslem inhabitants in parts of the USSR who, on being told that there are no *Shaitans*, consider such reassurances to be nonsense since they kept meeting the creatures.

And Serikova, the technical-zoologist woman who, terrified

when she suddenly saw an Almas squatting cross-armed a yard from her bed, explained in her subsequent report that, though at the time she did cry out the name of the Lord, she was really no God-Believer.

Some accounts though do raise pity and wonder at the incongruity and cruelty of some of the earth's unexplainable factors, as when the *Almas*, shot in the foot, reacted in a pain and fear almost human, and went whimpering and limping away in shock and surprise.

And there are unforgettable refinements of callous inhumanity caused through ignorance, as revealed in records of the ancient oriental practices of hunting these poor half-humans to slaughter them for "Wild Man Medicine".

Compassion stirs at the story of the tame *Almas* woman who attached herself to the young farmer, Kardanov, and the strangest story of all, the story of Zana. Zana, who from her savage ferocity and fury grew tame, became part of a household and responded only to her master's commands. Who played with stones like a child or, the Neanderthaler, would tear down a whole vine to gorge on grapes. Whose grandchildren are still alive, and normal human beings.

What savage dreams or images passed behind the near-animal mind of Zana when she lay in the deep sleep coma induced by long draughts of wine? It is an extraordinary picture, and the humanity of her descendants even more extraordinary, both psychologically and biologically.

Surely there was, or is, a groping flicker of the human feeling in the dark minds of those half-humans. The thought of their current existence fills one with wonder and speculation.

The deeper one probes the reason for this strange mystery, the more some tentative conclusions take shape.

There are not just three or four species of an unidentified anthropoid. The Snowman or Yeti or any other name that identifies him is but one very rare sub-human species of as many varied appearances as we have. He is a rare survivor hiding in the wilder places from the rest of humanity.

Facts can be unpalatable. "*As I came closer still I found it was my brother."*

We are launching out into marvels of space exploration while still not knowing everything about our own planet.

I may be verbally flayed for what I am about to say but perhaps after all we are not meant to discover the whole truth about the Snowman, Yeti, *Almas* or Hairy Man.

Perhaps these are the primal rough and secret stock preserved to withstand and survive any final disaster, preserved and hidden as the raw material for a fresh start in evolution should we finally blow up our so-called civilisation.

There is more to all living humanity than flesh and bones and potential "spare parts".

The Spirit that always walked on the face of the waters remains.

A List of Names and Terms so far Identified throughout the World as possibly Denoting Various Types of "Remnant Hominids"

GORDON CREIGHTON

NOTE: Most reports of the "remnant hominids" or "human relics" come at present from the Eurasian land-mass. This region is a vast ethnological and linguistic mosaic. There are, for example, at least 127 different languages in the Soviet Union alone. And it was not until 1958, when the Russians commenced their serious and systematic study of the "Snow-Man Problem", that their scholars realised how widespread throughout the whole area were the traditions of the existence of such creatures and how numerous were the names given to them in the various languages. No doubt there are still many more names that have not yet come to light. This list contains 131!

1. ACCEPTED OR PROPOSED SCIENTIFIC NAMES

Homo Neanderthalensis ("Neanderthal Man").
Homo Nocturnus ("Nocturnal Man") (Linnaeus).
Homo Troglodytes ("Cave Man") (Linnaeus).
Primihomo Asiaticus (suggested by V. A. Khakhlov).
Dinantropoides Nivalis ("Abominable Snow Anthropoid") (suggested by Professor Bernard Heuvelmans).

2. ENGLISH NAMES

Abominable Snowman.
Snowman.
Bigfoot.   California.

Wudéwásá. ⎱ Wuduwasa. ⎰ Wudewas.	Old Anglo-Saxon name, from a XVth century English Bestiary. Meaning: "Wood-Man". (From it are believed to derive the English surnames Wood*house* and W*odehouse*, via the forms: Wodwos; Wodewese; Wodewose; Wodwose; Woodwose.)

3. INDIAN NAMES OF NORTH AND SOUTH AMERICA

Sasquatch Giant.	British Columbia, Canada.
Sasquatch.	
Oh-Ma (Big Foot).	California.
Soquwiam.	Name used by Chehalis Indians.
Seeahtik.	Name used by Canadian Indians.
Wauk-Wauk.	„ „ „
Te Sami'etl Soquiam.	„ „ „
Saskehavis.	„ „ „
Wendigo.	„ „ „
Wentigo.	„ „ „
Whitico.	„ „ „
"Ice-Giants".	„ „ „
"Traverspine Apes".	„ „ „
Toonijuk.	Eskimo name on Baffin Island and north from there to Greenland. Further west the Eskimos have several other similar names.
Maricoxi.	Indian name, reported by Col. Fawcett from Matto Grosso area of Brazil.
Shiru.	A hairy pigmy on the eastern slopes of the north Andean Massif in Colombia and Ecuador.
Didi.	Large hairy hominid in the Guiana Massif.

4. AFRICAN NAMES

Chemosit. ⎱ Nandi Bear. ⎰	Names used in East Africa, in the languages of the Elgeyo and Nandi tribes.

174

Kereite.
Ngoloko.

5. INDIAN NAMES

Ban Manas. }
Van Manas. }   Meaning: "Forest Man", in languages derived from Sanskrit. Garwhal, N. India.

Bang.
Bangjakri.
Rakshasa.   (Mythical.) Sanskrit term for *Demon*.

6. MALAYAN AND INDONESIAN NAMES

Trolak Ape-Man.   Malaya.
Orang Batek.
Orang Pendek.   Meaning: "Short or Stocky Man" in Malay language (name used in Sumatra).
Sedapa.   Name used in Sumatra.
Sindai.   Name used in Sumatra.
Beruang Rambai.   Name used in Sarawak. Meaning, in Dyak language, "Long-Haired Bear".

7. TIBETAN, NEPALESE, SIKKIMESE, AND BHUTANESE NAMES

Mi-Gö.   Usual, current name in these countries. Meaning: "Wild Man".

Mighu.   Local pronunciation in Bhutan for Tibetan *Mi-Gö*.

Kang-Mi.   Meaning in Tibetan: "Snow Man".

Metch-Kangmi. }
Metoh-Kangmi. }   Dubious. Probably corrupt.

Rakshi-Bompo.   A Tibetan/Sanskrit hybrid word. Meaning: "Powerful Demon".

Dre-Mo.   Meaning in Tibetan: "Female Demon". (There is, however, confusion with a somewhat similar Tibetan word meaning a *she-bear*).

Yeh-Teh. Yeti.	Said to be pronounced "Yeh-Tay". Meaning and origin not established. Yeti seems today to be the usual word employed in Nepal by Newari-speaking Nepalese (i.e. those who do not speak Tibetan but the national language).
Mi-Chhem-Po.	Meaning in Tibetan: "Big Man".
Mi-Bom-Po.	„ „ „ "Powerful Man".
Dzu-Teh.	Said to be a word of the Lepcha language.
Sandja.	Said to be a Tibetan word. Not identified.
Srin-Po.	(Mythical.) Meaning: "Man-Eating Demon". (Identical with the Sanskrit *Rakshasa*).
Harrum-Mo.	Said to be a man in the Lepcha language. Unidentified.
Me-Teh.	Unidentified.
Chu-Teh.	Probably same as Dzu-Teh.
Sogpa.	Not identified.
Nyalmo.	„ „
Teh-Lma.	„ „
Chutey.	See Dzu-Teh or Chu-Teh. (Unidentified.)
Mihteh.	Probably same as Me-Teh. (Unidentified.)

7. CHINESE NAMES

Hsüeh-Jen.	Normal current term used in newspapers, etc. Meaning, in Chinese language: "Snow Man".
Mao-Jen.	Term used in some provinces. Meaning in Chinese language: "Hairy Man".
Mo-Zhyn.	Same as Mao-Jen, but as pronounced in the language of the Muslim minority people known as Tungans, Dungans or Hui-Hui, of whom small pockets are found both in China and USSR.
Jen-Hsiung.	Term used in Shensi Province and elsewhere. Meaning in Chinese language: "Man-Bear".

Hsing-Hsing.	An old term, nowadays used only to denote "ape", but evidently used in former centuries to denote the Yeti or Snowman.
P'i. } P'ei.}	Variant pronunciations given in old dictionaries for an extremely rare and now obsolete Chinese character which seems to have been used at various times in the past to denote either the Japanese Brown Bear (*Ursus Arctos*) or the Yeti.

9. MONGOLIAN NAMES

Almas.	The normal current term used today in newspapers and books. Also has a subsidiary meaning of *demon, sorcerer,* or *witch.*
Nühni Almas.	Meaning in Mongolian language: "Burrow-Almas", and indicative of caves or burrows as habitat.
Dzagin Emgen.	Meaning in Mongolian language: "Old Woman of the Saxaul Thickets" and denoting female Almas.
Dzagin Almas.	Meaning "Almas of the Saxaul Thickets".
Hün Göröös.	Meaning in Mongolian language: "Man-Beast".
Hün Har Göröös.	Meaning in Mongolian language: "Black Man-Beast".
Zerleg Hün.	Meaning in Mongolian language: "Wild Man."

10. NAMES USED IN THE SOVIET UNION

Snezhnyy Chelovek.	The normal current Russian term used used in newspapers, books, etc. Meaning: "Snow Man".

Almast.   Another term used widely in Russian documents. Presumably derived from Mongolian word *Almas* or from a similar word in one of the numerous Tartar or Mongolian languages.

11. THE MISCELLANEOUS NAMES FOUND SO FAR AMONG THE NON-RUSSIAN PEOPLES OF THE SOVIET UNION

Abanauayu.   Meaning: "Forest Man". Language: Abkhazian (Caucasus Region of U.S.S.R.).

Abasy.   Meaning and language not ascertained. Far N.E. Siberia.

Adam-Dzhapais.   Meaning: "Wild Man". Language: Kirghizian. (Pamirs, Kirghiz Republic of U.S.S.R., etc.)

Adam-Japais.   Variant of preceding.

Adam-Yavei.   Language not identified. Probable meaning: "Wild Man".

Adzhina.   Name found in Pamir Mountains. Language and meaning not ascertained.

Albast.   A word cognate with *Almas* and *Almast*. Language: Kazakh. (Kazakh Republic of U.S.S.R. and elsewhere, among pockets of Kazakh nomads.)

Alboost.   See *Albast*.

Biaban-Guli. } Bianbanguli. }   Terms found in Azerbaijan Republic, Caucasus area of U.S.S.R. Language and meaning not ascertained.

Chuchuna.   Term used in far N.E. Siberia. Language: Yakut. Meaning not ascertained.

Dev.   Name widely used by Tadjik-speaking people in Pamir Mts. and vicinity. Meaning in Tadjik language: "*Devil; demon; unclean spirit*". (An Indo-European

LIST OF NAMES AND TERMS

word, cognate with our English word
devil.)

Dzehez-Tyrmak.	A term used in the Pamir Mts. Language and meaning not ascertained.
Farishta.	Term used in the Pamirs. Language and meaning not ascertained.
Galubyavan.	Meaning: "Wild Man". Pamir Mts. and possibly other areas of U.S.S.R. Also Afghanistan. Language not ascertained.
Gubganana.	Term used in Kabardinian language, in Caucasus Mts., to denote the *female Yeti*.
Gul'biyavan.	Meaning: "Wild Man". Pamir Mts. and also Afghanistan. No doubt dialect form of or cognate with preceding. Language not ascertained.
Gulebaney.	Term used to denote *male Yeti* in area of Talysh Mts., Azerbaijan Republic, in the Caucasus. Language not ascertained, probably Azerbaijani, and meaning probably "Wild Man".
Golub-Yavan. Guli-B'yabon. Gulibyavan. Gul'bi-Yavan.	Variant forms of above, meaning "Wild Man". (Turkish language: *Yavani*, wild.)
Kaptar.	Term used in Azerbaijan and Daghestan (Caucasus Mts. area of the U.S.S.R.). Precise meaning not ascertained.
Keetar.	Term used in Caucasus. Language and meaning not ascertained.
Kheed'eki.	Term used in Verkhoyan'e area of Far N.E. Siberia. Probably Yakut language.
Kiik-Kish.	Term used in Kirghiz Republic and among Kirghiz nomads. Meaning in Kirghiz language: "Wild Man".
Kiik-Adam.	Term used in Kazakhstan Republic and among nomad Kazakhs. Meaning in Kazakh language: "Wild Man".

179

Kish-Kiik.	Term used in Kirghiz Republic and among nomad Kirghiz. Meaning: "Wild Man".
Kshy-Kiik.	Variant of preceding.
Ksii-Gyik. Kishi-Kiyik. Ksy-Gyik. }	Kazakh and Kirghiz variants. "Wild Man".
Kuchena. Kuchuna. }	Terms used in Verkhoyan'e region of Far N.E. Siberia. Language probably Yakut. Meaning not ascertained. (See *Chuchuna*.)
Kulieybani.	Talysh Mts., Azerbaijan Republic, in Caucasus Mts. Seemingly yet another variant of *Galubyavan*: "Wild Man".
Meshe-Adam.	Daghestan? (Caucasus Mts. area). Meaning: "Wild Man".
Mulen. Mulena. }	Terms used in Far N.E. Siberia. Language and meaning not ascertained.
Nasua.	Term used by Tadjiks of Tadjik Republic, Pamir Mts. region. Meaning: "Wild Man".
Ochokochi.	Term used in the Mingrelian language. (One of the languages of the Georgian Republic in the Caucasus.) Precise meaning not ascertained.
Pare. Peri. }	Terms used in Pamir Mts. area. Language not ascertained. Meaning: "*Demon, devil, or evil spirit*".
Shaitan.	Term widely used by Muslim peoples of the U.S.S.R. to denote the Yeti. Meaning: "*Satan, Devil, Demon*".
Tkhis-Katsi	Term used in the Caucasus region. Language and precise meaning not ascertained. Probably Georgian, in which language, *Katsi*="*man*", and *Tkhis*="*goat*".
Vil'moshin'.	Term used in Talysh Mts. area of Azer-

baijan Republic in Caucasus to denote the *female Yeti*. Precise meaning and language not ascertained.

Yabalyk-Adam.
Term used in Pamir Mts. region. Language not identified. Presumable meaning: "Wild Man".

Yaboy-Adam.⎫
Yavo-Khal'g. ⎭
Terms used in Pamir Mts. region. Presumably variants of preceding term.

Voyt.
Term used somewhere in U.S.S.R. Precisely where, or language, or meaning not ascertained.

Zhabayy Adam.
Term used in Kazakh Republic and among Kazakh nomads. Meaning in Kazakh language: "Wild Man".

Zhapayy Kishi.
Term used in Kirghiz Republic and among Kirghiz nomads. Meaning in Kirghiz language: "Wild Man".

Index